Beyond the
Apple Orchard

Beyond the
Apple Orchard

Dolly Withrow

Elk River Press

Elk River Press
Charleston, WV

10 9 8 7 6 5 4 3 2 1

Printed in USA

Library of Congress Number : 2003113649

ISBN : 0-9710389-3-7

Book Design and Front Cover Photograph:
Colleen Anderson

Many of the essays in this book were originally aired on
WV Public Radio and published in the *Jackson Herald* and
the *Charleston Daily Mail*.

Distributed by:
Pictorial Histories Distribution
1416 Quarrier Street
Charleston, WV 25301
www.wvbookco.com

Table of Contents

II. REFLECTIONS

III. RINGSIDE

Preface

The most frequently asked question at my signings in bookstores is "What is your book about?" The answer for both *More than Penny Candy* and this book is the same. I have written a collection of short takes on life in both the past and the present. The topics are varied and wide-ranging, but the brief "stories" are true or represent my "take" on today's world. Some scholars call what I write creative nonfiction. *Beyond the Apple Orchard* is nonfiction in that I have not created stories out of pure imagination. The events are real. They did happen, although for narrative enhancement, I have used some of the devices from the fiction writer's toolbox. The core of each experience, however, has been left intact.

This book is divided into three parts. Part I, "Remembrances," comprises stories of life in the '40s and '50s, although a few pieces include current experiences that have triggered memories of past years. The first section begins with "In My Grandfather's House," which sets the stage for life on Brickyard Hill during the '40s. I have ordered the stories so that one experience leads logically into the next. One reader has said that the first section reads like a novel. I have used vivid descriptions, dialogue, and setting—all for the reader's pleasure. Part I also contains "A Soldier's Story," which takes place at the beginning of World War II. True tales about high school graduation, visits to county fairs, first dance experiences, and that initial trip away from home will undoubtedly spark the reader's own memories of similar events. Part I offers a genuine portrait of a culture that is long gone and will never be again. Teachers have purchased my first collection to share yesteryear's culture with their students. A Maryland teacher, though, has said that because of the descriptive prose she uses *More than Penny Candy* in her creative writing class. This book continues the same style and format as that of *More than Penny Candy* but offers all new experiences.

Part II, "Reflections," is made up of musings about the night sky and sunsets; the latter is used metaphorically as well as literally. I included a profile of an "older" student who sat in my literature class many years earlier and a piece that was inspired by two black and white photographs on a doctor's waiting room wall, photographs that reminded me of the uniformity that veneers our nation from coast to coast. There are many other topics, including pieces about nature and human nature and pets and country living. The second part is what I hope will be for the reader a thought-provoking section of *Beyond the Apple Orchard*.

Part III is titled "Ringside." The title means that, you, the reader will sit ringside in a symbolic seat that provides a close-up view of life's hilarious spectacles. This section covers today's many quirky sideshows in our society. For example, "Studies and Half Studies" focuses on research conducted by scientists—research that indicates a man listens with only half a brain. I add that often a woman chats with only half a brain, which makes for poor communication between men and women. From our nationwide obsession with physical fitness to the aging process, from snoring to cooking to earning the DDDD (doctoral degree in deciphering directions), I've covered the breadth and depth of our society's spectacles.

Beyond the Apple Orchard offers something for readers of every age. As always, my intention has been to entertain first. When I hear that my work has both entertained and inspired and that buyers have returned to purchase more copies of my book for gifts, I am humbled and gratified. No author could ask for more.

It is my hope that you will enjoy each "story" and then will share your thoughts with friends and family. Thank you for reading my book.

~Dolly Withrow

REMEMBRANCES

In My Grandfather's House

He wore faded black trousers of an old suit that through the years had become threadbare. The pants, like him, had at one time been young and handsome. I watched him amble from the garden, his bowed legs moving carefully as he approached our front porch. Before stepping onto the concrete, he stomped his feet to remove any residue of dusty clay from leather shoes, the laces of which had long been lost. At one time the shoes, like his shirt and trousers, were reserved strictly for funerals and church services, but in their final days they served another purpose. A tattered fedora with a hole in the front crease completed his gardening apparel.

After moving into the shade of the porch, he pulled from his shoulders wide gray suspenders that hung below his waist like saddlebags. He unbuttoned and removed his yellowed dress shirt. His back was stooped from years of hard work. His crimson cheeks, along with his tanned forearms and hands, gave the only indications of long hours he endured under the hot sun as he bent over his hoe. Each summer he worked to coax the reluctant red clay to do his bidding. It did.

Charlie Bird Frame, my maternal grandfather, had no water hose, no plow, and no horse. His meager tools consisted of a hoe, a rake, and two buckets. During dry days, he drew water from a well in our yard, filled the buckets, and carried them to his parched garden. He hoed around his corn to break up constantly forming clods. Never using pesticides, he painstakingly picked

Charlie Bird and Elmira Frame, the author's grandparents.

hungry bugs from the underside of leaves. During both
World War II and for years afterwards, our garden sup-
plied a bounty of food. From my grandfather's garden,
we harvested corn, green beans, onions, leaf lettuce, and
tomatoes, all of which he shared with passersby or
neighbors.

Despite being a hard worker even in his seventies,
my grandfather had a sense of humor. He was a practical joker but not in a mean sense. I remember one morn-

ing as I was getting ready to go to work at a local bank I shoved my foot down into a high-heeled shoe only to find the toe had been stuffed with, of all things, marbles. I can still see my grandfather laughing. Unlike my grandmother, who attended church whenever she was able and read her Bible every day, my grandfather attended church only occasionally. I don't recall his ever reading the Bible. My grandmother quoted verses to him so often that I guess he saw no need.

Still, he was a generous man, something I never thought about at the time. He opened his home to anyone who needed shelter. Aunts and uncles moved in and out with their spouses, the moves depending on each one's twist of fortune. My grandmother's brother lived with us for a time. I remember once that an entire family visited us from New York City, which we thought was in another world. The couple had many children of all ages, and they slept on the floor of a house that was sometimes almost empty and at other times filled with family members. Before moving to New York, the visiting family had lived across the ravine and on a distant hill facing our house. The couple left West Virginia so the husband could find gainful employment. Their dialect had already begun to change when they returned for a visit. I remember how fast they talked; their words were clipped and curt.

When visitors left and the house grew still, my grandfather wrote in a tiny red notebook. He kept a record of the weather and I wondered why. Now, to my own surprise, I sometimes write in my journal a report of the day's weather. On one September day, I wrote, " It is cool with pale sunshine filtering through clouds. The shadows grow long, and darkness comes early." On that day, I remembered and mimicked my Grandfather Frame.

Finding Our Own Way

"Though nothing can bring back the hour
Of splendour in the grass, of glory in the flower;
We will grieve not, rather find
Strength in what remains behind;
In the primal sympathy
Which having been must ever be;
In the soothing thoughts that spring
Out of human suffering;
In the faith that looks through death,
In years that bring the philosophic mind."

~William Wordsworth

As the scarlet sun dropped behind the western hill, dusk gave way to night. I was anticipating an evening of fun as I watched the moon appear. Round and yellow, it hung low in the autumn sky. Standing on our front porch, I looked beyond the darkened road and down the sloping field toward the house where some of my childhood friends lived. I watched for Rosie and Barbara to come out their door. It was not long before I saw their door open and a rectangle of light spill across their back porch. I watched their silhouettes as they left the house. I then crossed the road and descended the hill. That evening, we were going to build a fire, for the air was already giving a hint of winter's chill.

When snow covered the ground, that hillside provided a place for sledding. During the summer, in that same field, we caught lightning bugs and put them in jars with metal lids into which we had punched small holes. On that moonlit evening in late fall, the ground was still damp from a recent rain. Our field was soon bustling with activity. The neighborhood boys built, with small tree limbs, a fire around which as many as ten or twelve of us kids sat cross-legged. Forming an unbreakable circle, we watched light and shadow play across one another's young faces. We each had brought a potato from home, and later, when the fire began to die, we buried it deep beneath the glowing embers. There were no marshmallows, no wieners. Those would have been luxuries, and we did not have luxuries.

We had something far more precious. Without computers or PlayStations or cell phones, we learned how to survive. Without organized games led by adults, we were given space and freedom and opportunities to find our own way. We learned how to be individuals, how to create our own entertainment. As dark smoke swirled upward and changed directions, we shifted positions to prevent smoke from getting in our eyes. We told ghost stories and shared dreams and sometimes expressed our fears. There were quiet times as well—times when we just stared into the reddish-orange flames, each holding private feelings within the chambers of the heart. Late in the night, we doused the embers with buckets of water and each headed toward home while looking forward to a new day of carefree play.

Those of us who sat around that small fire many years ago cannot bring back the hour of our youth, but we do not mourn. As Wordsworth has so beautifully reminded us in his poem, "Ode: Intimations of Immortality from Recollections of Early Childhood," we have been left with strength and philosophic minds and, yes, our own recollections of childhood.

Beyond the Apple Orchard

Up by seven on a warm summer morning, I was cheered by the golden sunlight already sweeping the hills around our home. After eating breakfast and packing a lunch of peanut butter and jelly sandwiches, I waited impatiently for Barbara, Rosie, Phoebe, and Erma to stop by the house. They made up most of our childhood gang, although sometimes older sisters joined us. We were each around ten years old, more or less, and being that age is to know something of enchantment. We were always eager to talk and dream about our future. The apple orchard was one of our special places, offering a beautiful bower, secluded and private.

By mid-morning on that summer day, my friends and I began our climb up the steep, twisting path that led from our back porch to a plateau where four apple trees stood like sentinels on the corners of a small square of sloping land. The limbs overhead, lush with foliage, provided a domed roof through which sunlight and shadow danced in constant movement on the moss-covered ground. As we sat in a circle on nature's green carpet and time passed lazily by, we ate our sandwiches and talked about movie stars and magical places farther up yet other hills behind us, places filled with mystery and adventure. Such is the world of a ten-year-old. And we talked about boys and our future and about whoever failed to be with us at any given time. We laid bare our dreams, our fears, and our hopes as we confided in one another.

Sitting in our circle, Pheobe suddenly pointed to her right and yelled, "Look! Look over there."

As our heads whipped around in the direction she indicated, we saw a dead sparrow lying in the dark shade. The lifeless bird gave us a purpose for that day.

We would give the creature a proper funeral; it deserved no less.

Later, back in the kitchen of my home, we found a large matchbox. After lining the box with cotton fabric, printed with faded bluebells, we ascended the hill once more. Using a sharp rock, we took turns digging a shallow grave at the foot of the tree where we had found the sparrow.

Placing the corpse in its special coffin, we softly repeated strange words we had heard but with which we had little real acquaintance.

"From ashes to ashes and dust to dust," we muttered.

Since that day many years ago, we have each climbed most of the steep, twisted path that life offers to all humans. We have now learned the meaning of those words we uttered in the innocent space of childhood when we had more future than past, those now being reversed. We have learned that some paths we can choose for ourselves. No matter what our choices might be, though, we have learned that other paths—perhaps steeper and rougher—are nonetheless paths chosen for us.

The five of us have survived, those of us who sat years ago in that apple orchard where sun and shadow danced at our feet. One friend has lost her husband to death. Two friends have lost their husbands to divorce, and still another friend has lost both her husband and a son to death. Most of us have remained in the emerald green hills of West Virginia. One, though, lives in Michigan and has lost her Southern accent, but we still speak the same language. I remember those days when we dreamed of a future so distant we thought it would never arrive, a future that has now mostly passed.

A Soldier's Story

In black ink someone has written on the bottom of a yellowed snapshot, "about 1942." The photograph shows two people on the front porch of my childhood home. I see myself in the picture as a young girl squinting into the afternoon sun. Smiling, I wear the innocent face of youth. My faded dress hangs loosely from the shoulders, and my dark hair, shoulder-length, is held back with bobby pins. The other image is of Ray Frame, my first cousin. His khaki shirt and pants are part of his United States Army uniform. Despite our posing for the now unknown photographer, my cousin wears a look of concern without even a hint of a smile.

Before World War II, Ray worked in Civilian Conservation Corps (CCC) camps, which were part of President Franklin D. Roosevelt's efforts to pull our nation out of the Great Depression. Later, Ray worked for the Nehi Bottling Company. Sometimes, he would bring samples home, and my favorites were the chocolate- and strawberry-flavored drinks. We made a hide-and-seek game of the Nehi products. He would hide them, and I'd seek. Like an older brother, he helped to mold me into the person I am today. Ray valued a formal education, although his own was halted early in life. When I had a cold and didn't want to walk to Grandview Grade School, he gave me a handkerchief and a box of Smith Brothers licorice cough drops, then shoved me out the door. Often, the snow was deep and the temperature frigid. None of that mattered, for he wouldn't listen to my whining. Because of Ray, I learned early in life that I would have to do many things I didn't like in order to achieve future goals.

I can't remember the first time I saw Ray, but I do know the story that family members told about him.

The author and her cousin, Ray Frame.

When his mother, Inez Jane, died, he was only eleven years old, and he stood at the foot of her bed, crying. He asked, "Who will patch my pants now?"

Left an orphan, he then came to live with his grandparents (and mine) in the stucco house on Brickyard Hill. Industrious, he grew up to open a small grocery store at the foot of our hill, but that didn't last long because vandals destroyed everything he had. After that, he gave up trying to own a business, and for the rest of his life, worked for someone else.

Soon after December 7, 1941, Ray announced that he was going to join the Army, that he was needed. He boarded a red city bus and rode to Charleston, West

Virginia, where he joined to fight for a worthwhile cause. He was a member of that generation Tom Brokaw has called "the greatest," and Ray deserved the label. No one gave a rat's ankle about the self-esteem of folks in his tough times. In fact, his generation was made up of individuals who wouldn't know what to think of a future generation whose greatest concern would be buying clothing with designer labels.

When in service, Ray wrote in every letter that he couldn't tell us his whereabouts or where he was going. News reporters didn't feel it was our right to know. War demanded secrets, and men and women in service knew how to keep them. Our family never knew what Ray endured in the war, for typical of people during his time, he was not a whiner. I do remember, though, that he came home with ribbons and medals and an all-expense paid rest after his honorable discharge. He left home for Miami, Florida, and never returned to West Virginia except for one short visit with his wife and family.

Oh, yes, the yellowed photograph also depicts two dogs on the porch, Spot and Fido. Along with my dear cousin, they're all gone now. All that remains is the old house where the ghosts of many stories continue to linger.

Decoration Day

Excited about the day ahead, I was outside early enough to see tiny beads of dew clinging to the grass beside the well in our yard. Each drop shone like a diamond in the early morning shimmer of sunlight. I smelled the aroma of red and white roses clustered on large bushes in our yard, the branches—heavy with blooms—drooping earthward. On the front porch, a rake, hoe and sickle leaned against the wall of our house.

It was late May many years ago, just before Decoration Day. The garden tools on the porch were clues to our anticipated activities. Seeing those tools waiting like silent soldiers, I knew that shortly after eating breakfast, my mother, Aunt Sissy, Aunt Ocie and I would soon make our pilgrimage to Sattes Cemetery. Out of six gravesites, just one was occupied in our family's plot. It held Inez Jane, who was the late sister of my mother and Aunt Sissy. She had died at 32 of tuberculosis, leaving her eleven-year-old son, my cousin Ray.

Between our house and the graveyard stood a church built of yellow tiles. The Prayer and Faith Tabernacle provided a link between the living and the dead, between our house and the cemetery. It was a place where the living prepared for life after death. In those innocent days of childhood, though, I knew little about such links between the now and hereafter.

I did know about cemeteries and how hard we worked each May as we cut weeds, raked them over the hill, and placed fresh roses at the head and foot of Inez Jane's grave. Now, the older I get, the more I realize that much of what sets us humans apart, much of what makes us more humane, is the care we continue to give to the resting places of loved ones who are no longer with us.

Since that day so long ago, Decoration Day has become Memorial Day, a time now for picnics and family get-togethers. But the biggest change for those of us who have ancestors reposed in Sattes is in the graveyard itself. Of course, Sattes never resembled the modern-day cemeteries where the land, carpeted with grass, is as level as a living room floor, where markers have special places for inserting flowers. No, that was never Sattes.

Rather, in the scant four acres that make up Sattes, each family's plot was different. Some plots were surrounded by chain-link fences, others by borders of grass, and still others by wrought iron fences. Each was unique. Most veterans' graves boasted tiny red, white, and blue American flags rippling in the spring breeze. Just as the veterans had in life supported all that the flag symbolizes, their graves supported the symbol itself. Those flags were fitting tributes to those who had given their lives so that we might live in freedom.

When we neighbors made our yearly journeys to clean and decorate graves, we also visited one another beneath blue spring skies. As warm winds whipped skirts about the women and blew straw hats back from the men's sun-lined faces, they found time to inquire about a grandmother, to ask how she had endured the winter with her rheumatism. Leaning on rakes, they might ask a neighbor whether she had heard from her son who had married and moved out of state. They could catch up on news that had remained unavailable during cold winter days.

Today the cemetery has changed. There is no access to Sattes Cemetery in North Charleston. Standard Brick Road has been closed by the city government, and the right-of-way shown on a map has disappeared on the land itself. The graves of my grandparents and four aunts remain weed-infested because we no longer have access to them. Still, on early May mornings when dewdrops glisten in the sun, I yearn again to place live roses on six graves in North Charleston, West Virginia.

Celebrating Freedom

It was the Fourth of July and hot wind whipped my long hair straight back as I stood in the bed of our neighbor's black pickup truck, struggling to keep my balance. We rumbled along a two-lane paved highway for several miles. Then, after what seemed an eternity, we turned off onto a dusty dirt road that led to a large field with shade trees and plenty of grass for picnicking. Flowing nearby, a river with taffy-colored water offered a swimming hole. Once we arrived, all of us— the mother, father, their three sons and three daughters, and I—pitched in to help unload the truck. A zinc tub filled with ice held a huge watermelon. We unloaded the food and towels and a large blanket for spreading on the ground.

I was a skinny little girl, not more than ten or eleven, and under my blouse and shorts I wore a two-piece red bathing suit. The bottom had a slightly flared skirt, which I had chosen to hide my thin legs. Of course, it didn't work, but none of that mattered because while I had stood in the bed of that moving truck, facing the summer sun head-on, I thought I looked like a sultry movie star. I see young girls today with the same air I must have had then, and knowingly I smile. When we're children, imagination often replaces reality and even provides the oil that helps to smooth the rough places of childhood.

After we had unloaded the picnic supplies, we kids couldn't wait to hit the water. I had learned to swim earlier in the muddy waters of Two-Mile Creek near my Aunt Minerva's country house, so I was eager to jump in and swim like Esther Williams. (I was another movie star when I stood in the back of the truck.) Once in the river, I was Esther herself with a smiling face, hair braided and gelled to perfection, a one-piece bathing suit, and swim strokes that never ruffled the water. I carefully sliced the water with one slightly bent arm and hand turned sideways so as not to splash a single drop. Reality was another story, but I wasn't in a river; I was in Hollywood swimming in a gorgeous pool.

It was Independence Day, and I could be whoever and wherever I wanted to be as I paddled around— looking silly I'm sure—in that small brown river in my tiny corner of the world. In parts of the country, unknown to us, there were undoubtedly bands playing, speeches being made, and folks marching in parades, for the day was a celebration of our nation's birth date, July 4, 1776, when our infant nation declared its independence from Great Britain.

At the end of the day, tired and sunburned, we kids climbed back into the bed of the truck. It again rumbled along the dirt road, then onto the blacktop highway. Finally, we arrived back on Brickyard Hill where many families had displayed American flags. Revered as a symbol of freedom, the flag reminded us of those who had fought and of those who had died so that we might live in a country where we could grow up to be anything we wanted to be. As the sun slid behind the hill and a sliver of golden moon appeared in the night sky, my Grandfather Frame set off firecrackers. I listened to the loud pop of each tiny explosion and watched the small spray of yellow-orange sparks. I didn't realize it then, but the entire day had been about freedom in America.

A Sense of Place

As my mind meanders down the back roads of time, I know now that it was a strange juxtaposition. The Prayer and Faith Tabernacle stood high on a hill overlooking Cat Eye's beer joint. The owner's nickname was Cat Eye, and his beer parlor sat alongside Washington Street in North Charleston, West Virginia. Cat Eye's was housed in a one-story frame building that had been painted white. The owners lived in the back rooms.

On Saturday nights, the joint reverberated with jukebox music, loud talk, and raucous laughter. When I walked from my Grandmother Wood's house toward home on Brickyard Hill, I had to pass Cat Eye's. If it was late evening, I could hear the beat of country tunes and smell the stench of stale beer intermingled with cigarette smoke. A few minutes later, as I walked up the hill, if there was a revival in progress and if I listened carefully, I could hear echoing down from the Tabernacle the singing of hymns. Sometimes, I could hear clearly the words of "Amazing Grace" or "Just as I Am."

As odd as it may seem, many of the same people frequented both places at various times in their lives. My Grandfather Frame was a plainspoken man who in his old age stayed close to home. He went no farther from our house than to the grocery store at the foot of the hill. Still, he seemed to know everything about everybody in the neighborhood. Puffing his pipe as he sat on our front porch during hazy summer evenings, he often talked about folks who went to church when they needed to pray for something, but when things went well, he said they sat in the dark-varnished booths at Cat Eye's and drank beer. I know, though, that sometimes it went the other way, too. When troubles came, as they did much of the time, some of the troubled would seek alcohol as an escape, and Cat Eye's offered that temporary escape.

The owners of Cat Eye's had only one daughter. She was several years older than I was, and one day she told me that she would teach me how to dance. Now a girl of about eleven or twelve who had been wistfully watching her peers jitterbug was not about to turn down such an offer. And so on one late Saturday morning before the place was open for business, I was in Cat Eye's. The daughter was tall and thin with skin as pale as bleached parchment. She had blond hair and large blue eyes. She chose the tunes on the jukebox, and I discovered that I was quick to learn the rhythm and steps. Soon I was dancing with confidence at the USO.

I often taught my college students that we must write about what we know, that we must have a sense of place. There is little choice anyway, for how can we write about something we do not know? Writers in the Midwest write about the big sky and the flat land. Writers in the South write about swamplands and magnolias. Writers from New York City write about the sophistication of big-city life. Here in West Virginia, I write about juxtapositions, about the strange side-by-side contradictions that make up our state. It is about individuals who are as different from one another as snowflakes on a winter day. Outsiders who stereotype us as being of one culture are people who have no sense of place.

A Different Kind of Darkness

Morning classes at Grandview Grade School had gone well, but a tragedy, still hidden in the future, would make headline news around the world before day's end.

I remember during the morning our teacher stood in front of the room and read "Raggedy Ann" yet again. She loved the poem because she had a daughter named Ann, so we had to listen to the words almost every day. A short woman with a body as round as a blown-up balloon, she had spindly legs that nonetheless held her upright. Her face, the shape of a full moon, was accented with small lips that, throughout the day, retained layers of bright red lipstick. Her wire-rimmed glasses were topped with light brown hair that barely covered her ears. Fuzzy and permed to the max, her hair was parted to one side. Almond-shaped fingernails matched her lipstick. She must have been a good teacher, but the memory I carried away from her classroom, buried in the back corner of my mind, was of the day her half-slip fell to the floor. Not missing a beat, she bent over, picked it up, wadded it into a soft ball, then casually tossed it into the black metal wastebasket by the door. On that sunny day in the early '40s, we ate lunch in our classroom and then were dismissed to spend the remainder of the lunch hour on the playground.

The scene was typical of any grade schoolyard filled with active children. An observer even then, I watched as a few girls draped their legs over chinning bars and hung upside down, their long hair almost touching the ground. Smaller girls were on seesaws, rising into the air, then descending back to earth. Other students played London Bridge under shade trees at the yard's edge. Still others jumped rope. The high chain-link fence enclosed a sun-washed playground on that fateful day, and overhead the cloudless sky was the color of bluebonnets. It was a perfect day until. . . .

Like lightning striking, it happened so fast that no one was sure what had occurred. The explosion rocked the very earth beneath us; windows blew out of the school building, lying shattered on the ground. Kids ran toward the gate and were momentarily jammed in so they could barely move. The teachers could not escape from the schoolyard, for students were the faster runners. Our teacher climbed that chain-link fence and ran to her car. One girl, wearing braces on her teeth, simply jumped up and down, remaining in place as she screamed. I couldn't hear her screams because the roar of the fire and minor explosions overpowered all other sounds. Across the olive-brown waters of the Kanawha River, incredibly large clouds of orange-red fire rolled along the ground and then rolled toward the heavens. As I ran, the fire kept pace with me. It was as if fiery clouds had fallen from the sky and were covering all the earth.

Living in what was then called "the chemical center of the world" (whether it was or not), we were all aware of the dangers of an explosion. Knowing really little about chemicals, I still remember fearing the release of poison gases and the fear that the fire would ignite storage tanks holding other chemicals. We had heard many times that one blast could wipe out our entire valley.

Men lost their lives in that Carbide explosion, and other lives were forever altered. A day that had begun with laughter and sunshine ended with a different kind of darkness.

A Fair to Remember

As part of a large audience, I sat on bleachers under star-sprinkled skies. I could not see the stars, though, because of the large electric lights surrounding the grandstand and the open stage. I relaxed with friends on one of the middle bleachers and, at sixteen, I often had to stretch my neck to see the stage. Forming a constantly moving ring, night bugs buzzed and flitted around each light. The public address system crackled from time to time, but the performer's voice was clear enough that we could still hear her words.

Standing in front of the microphone, she said, "Howdee." She ended the word in a high-pitched tone. Then, she said, "I'm just so glad to be here, just so proud I could come."

Everyone knew her act was about to begin, and she received a long and hearty applause. She wore a long cotton dress with tiny red flowers and black leather shoes (sensible shoes, I think). Her trademark, though, was her flat straw hat, adorned with fake flowers and a single price tag that dangled from the brim. The one and only Minnie Pearl was about to entertain us with her special brand of monologue.

The 4-H fair was held each fall in our area, and my Aunt Phyllis worked for the 4-H. She had an office and was, in my young mind, a woman of influence on the fairgrounds. She was in charge of the ribbons that would be offered to winners in various categories. Some would receive awards for the best pies or the best quilts or maybe the finest goat.

Each year a carnival accompanied the fair and its exhibits. Rides and sideshows and games of chance were all part of the colorful scene. There were rides that turned us upside down and others that looped and circled. We could enjoy the Ferris wheel or swings that suspended us out over the crowds.

The sideshows were as politically incorrect as anything I remember of those post-World War II years. The ten-foot tall painted picture of a bearded lady adorned the side of one tent. Outside another tent, a hawker yelled, "Come one, come all. See the fattest man on earth." Still another would yell, "Come inside and see the two-headed baby" or "the wild man from Borneo."

A man dressed in a glittery tuxedo swallowed the fire from a flaming sword. We pitched pennies, trying to land them in carnival dishes. Or we shot guns at yellow duck decoys that moved rapidly along a trough of water at the back of a tent. There were men who would guess our weight or age, all for a price. There was a test of strength as we tried to maneuver a huge rubber hammer to make the ball go to the top of a pole and ring a bell.

During the year Minnie Pearl was the star attraction, I had a job at the fair. I worked under the grandstand in a booth sponsored by Charleston Wholesale Grocer. My job was to serve samples of Golden Dream coffee in white paper cups shaped like tiny cones. My booth was popular, and I know now that all those folks already had golden dreams of their own, even as I did.

Now, on starry nights, I know it was a fair to remember.

A Dream Dancing

Stained and yellowed with age, a receipt from St. Francis Hospital is dated August 30, 1939. The receipt itemizes the costs of my tonsillectomy, and they total only $15. The paper, as fragile as ancient parchment, ushers in a flood of memories.

I remember a two-story white house on Charleston's West Side. After my operation, I was brought to that house, owned by Cora Belle Wood, my paternal grandmother. I was placed on a Victorian sofa in the parlor to

Aunt Phyllis.

the left of the entry hall. The room boasted matching chairs, a fireplace, a hardwood floor, marble-topped tables, and a bay window adorned with lace curtains.

My Aunt Phyllis, who was then a young widow, entertained me as I took tiny bites of vanilla ice cream, my throat burning with each swallow. Wearing a floor-length gown of black velvet, my aunt swirled around the room, singing, "Did you ever see a dream walking? Well, I did."

She had blond hair, blue eyes, and skin as fair as a summer day. Although I was a mere child, it was clear to me that she saw herself as a dream walking. During the ensuing years, she would play an important role in my life. When I graduated from college in my forties, she gave me a gift, and like all her gifts, it was unusual. Inside a hollow cat of clear glass was a pale yellow canary made of plastic. My aunt had fashioned a bow tie from a one-hundred dollar bill and placed it around the cat's neck. Oh, yes, the cat wore a sheepish grin.

When my Grandmother Wood died, my aunt inherited the house on the West Side, but by that time she had remarried. She and her husband bought a house on a hillside that overlooked downtown Charleston. She was excited about her find—a country place right in the middle of the city, she had said. The house was made of textured building blocks, the color of putty, but both inside and out, the house soon revealed my aunt's unique decorating taste. Following her instructions, my Uncle Bill painted the exterior shutters a dark teal green. He removed the steps from the front porch and closed the opening, leaving a porch that visitors could not enter. The back door was also made inaccessible because she asked Uncle Bill to screen in the small porch. The screen door remained locked from the inside. The third opening was an antiquated garage door that had never seen an automatic opener. In fact, the door opened from right to left. That, too, remained locked, but on the door was an old-fashioned bell that visitors could ring by turning a lever clockwise. If Aunt Phyllis chose to let them in, she would carefully descend dark, narrow stairs, work her way through a dank, dim basement, and open the garage door.

The upstairs had her signature everywhere. Reposing on my aunt's hearth, a marble lady lay on her side. A mirror so large it filled the entire wall behind her camel-back sofa had to be hung by professionals. The end wall, without windows, sported wallpaper with a fleur-de-lis background overlaid with a pattern of prominent blue flowers and huge red birds. The wall was then covered with pictures of all sorts, many of the frames having been made by my uncle. The effect was pure drama. At Christmas, Aunt Phyllis created a tree from what appeared to be water pipes. She painted them pink and placed pink ostrich feathers at the top. Long before anyone else was stringing tiny lights on bare-limbed trees in the winter, she did that.

She celebrated her last birthday in an assisted living home, sitting in a wheelchair beside her bed. She wore a ruffled beige blouse and matching slacks. Her son and my mother were there as I presented her with balloons and a plaid cotton robe in a wrapped box, gifts not as imaginative as hers had been. Telling her I would be back soon, I stayed for only a short time. That was the last time I saw her. A short time later, she died in a local hospital, but she had been years ahead of her time, an original. I can still see her, swirling around a room in a black velvet gown—a dream dancing.

One Star-Scattered Night

Wearing heavy layers of clothing and carrying a flashlight, I left our house and descended the three porch steps already piled high with frozen snow. Standing in the middle of the deserted road, I found myself in the midst of a vast white landscape. Everything was blanketed with snow as I looked at the night sky. There, I saw a canopy of brilliant stars. They appeared so close that I remember thinking if I could stretch my arms high enough I could almost touch them.

That January night in the late '40s was bitter cold. As I began high-stepping toward my Uncle Hobert's house, I listened to the crunch of snow with each step. That night years ago, I was a teenager and still had much to learn. Nonetheless, I was on a life-saving mission, and I felt important. My uncle had been to our house in the afternoon and asked me if I would attend a prayer service the church was having for Ollie, his wife.

She "had taken to her bed" because of a kidney ailment, and hospital stays had done little to alleviate her problem. My Aunt Ollie had been a quiet woman, even-tempered and kind. She had soft brown eyes and dark hair, which had just begun to turn gray. A flash of silver could occasionally be seen in her hair as she turned her head in the bright summer sun. But summer had passed, and for her, it might never return.

One day before that January night, I visited her. She looked at family members as they stood around her bed. World War II had ended several years earlier, but she was still in the middle of that war. When planes flew overhead, she thought they were Nazi bombers. Her fear was horrible to witness.

She screamed, "Don't you hear them? Get under the bed! They're going to bomb us."

Nightmares haunted her throughout her illness, and then one day she became so weak that my uncle feared he would lose her. That's when he asked me to attend the healing service.

Nearing my uncle's house, I saw the warm squares of yellow light in the windows. The cold of night had crept through my clothing, and I walked more quickly. As I entered the house, I saw that church members had already arrived. Perhaps as many as eight people were seated in the small bedroom. One special friend was there. He had prayed for my aunt during his weekly visits over the previous two months. An African-American, Mr. Taylor lived on Washington Street, below Brickyard Hill. I can still see him during his lone visits as he leaned back in his chair. He never bowed his head, but rather aimed his face toward the heavens, closed his eyes, and offered the most heart-rending prayers for my aunt's recovery. On this evening, though, we were all to kneel around her white iron bed and pray aloud in unison. It was the same way church members had prayed for my Aunt Sissy years earlier. Kneeling by Aunt Ollie's bed, I prayed longer than anyone else, and Ollie responded. I thought I must have had something special. I didn't, of course, and I would have been labeled vain by those good folks had they known of my conceit. My aunt, though, did appear to be lucid and stronger than she had been in months. She was never "out of her mind" again as my family said, and that was, according to those who prayed, the answer to their prayers. Later in that same month, on January 9, my Aunt Ollie died. Only forty-five years old, she said she was ready to go. Sometimes, prayers aren't answered in the way mere humans think they should be, so on January nights when I look at a clear sky, I still gaze at the stars and remember.

The Wandering Painter

It sat in a shadowy corner of our downstairs bedroom-living room combination. A wooden monstrosity, the large piano had been covered with a stain so dark that in the gloomy corner it appeared black. Both my mother and grandmother played the old piano "by ear." As one of them nimbly fingered the keys, hymns such as "The Old Rugged Cross" resounded throughout the two-story house. Because I was so young, I cannot recall the times they actually sat at its keyboard, but I know the kind of music my mother played years later when she had an opportunity. My memory holds only a vague image of our piano. The image appears to me as nothing more than a shattered fragment of a murky photograph. I do remember harboring a dream that one day I might take piano lessons. No one had ever mentioned such an idea, and I never voiced the wish.

Mother's youngest brother, my Uncle Edwin, made occasional visits to our Brickyard Hill home, a home owned by my maternal grandparents. During one such visit, Uncle Edwin ended any thoughts of piano lessons. He was a wanderer, a nomad. After many years, I now know that he was searching for something throughout his life, searching for something that, as far as I know, he never found. He roamed from place to place as he painted interiors and exteriors of houses. Talented and intelligent, he knew how to mix tints and hues to get the exact colors people preferred. I sometimes watched him as he studied color wheels he had placed on top of our claw-footed round table in the kitchen. One time, he tried to explain to me the mysteries involved in mixing two or more colors so that a new color would emerge.

His restlessness led him to drink alcohol, and it seemed that he couldn't survive without it. He often left houses only partially painted after receiving the first payment for his work. Whatever his dream was, he sought it in bottles of cheap wine and in strange towns, many far from home. His ceaseless wanderings took him to Cuba and Canada. I remember his talking about Havana, telling us that it was a beautiful city. More frequently, though, he meandered down streets and around curving roads in Ohio cities and small communities in his own West Virginia. He was as familiar with

Akron and Toledo as he was with Charleston, his hometown.

One summer day, I saw my uncle walking up the hill toward our home, his head and shoulders appearing first, like the tops of a ship's sails appearing first on the horizon. Uncle Edwin was a small-boned man with his black hair parted on the left side and swept back and to the right. His eyes, like our piano, were so dark as to appear almost black. They smoldered with an inner anger, an anger ignited by I knew not what. He had no teeth, but he could eat with ease raw vegetables or any other food. He had lost his teeth before I was born, so his toothless mouth looked natural to me. Sometimes, when he thirsted for "the drink," his temper became erratic. He was never at peace.

During that summer, a few days after I had watched him climb the hill toward home, he decided to take our piano apart. He was unable to get all the pieces back in place. The dismembered hulk formed a jagged stack in our side yard. I remember the dark wood glistening in the summer sun. Then, one day the old piano that had resided in our home for so many years had to be burned. My uncle, like the piano, is now gone, but I wonder what he could have been had he found his dream.

Moonlight and Gardenias

When I was a high school junior, I yearned to belong, to be popular like the majorettes and cheerleaders. Yearning to belong is an affliction that plagues the majority of teenagers, but I thought I was the only one so stricken.

While I excelled in English, shorthand, and typing,

I found science classes to be as befuddling as if I had encountered an extraterrestrial in my back yard. Our biology teacher could have been the prototype for the mad scientist. He wore rimless octagonal glasses as thick as crystal ashtrays. He sported a perpetual fiendish grin and a white lab coat that ended just above his shiny black shoes. One bright fall day he aimed a superior look at us and asked if anyone could tell him what the convex folds on the surface of the human brain were called. I frantically waved my hand in the air. Tilting his chin ever so slightly my way, he indicated I could answer. "They're called convulsions," said I.

The students who would one day become scientists snickered as my face burned crimson. To this day, I know those creases are called convolutions. I found algebra to be the most difficult subject of all. Why in the world would we call a number a letter? I was not in college prep, so I had to endure the subject for only a few short weeks.

My big chance to become one of the elite came one fine day when a classmate who viewed me as a linguistic peacock (she liked that) asked me to join a sorority. She hadn't heard about my linguistic feat in biology. I joined the organization and soon found myself sitting in an exclusive circle of girls who wore genuine angora sweaters, plaid skirts, and penny loafers with dimes in them. I was on the fund-raising committee, and we brainstormed. Someone said we could sell gardenias at the senior prom, which was to be held at a nightclub called the Casa Loma. Maybe the person who wanted to sell flowers had parents who owned a flower shop.

On a moonlit night of the prom, we four girls collectively owned a dozen open flat boxes filled with sweet-smelling gardenias. Each box had anchored to its sides the ends of a wide golden ribbon. At the nightclub in semi-darkness, we strolled among tables covered with white cloths. Seniors sat around tables and giggled as they nodded our way. We carried our rectangular boxes in front of us, hawking gardenias like movie stars wearing short outfits selling cigars and cigarettes in old movies. But we had a problem. The escorts who could afford corsages had already bought them. Those who couldn't afford them still couldn't.

I tried to hide in an alcove, but the senior sisters shoved me onto the floor first, and I was as embarrassed as the day I called convolutions, convulsions. When the evening mercifully ended, we had sold only three gardenias. The cream-colored petals of the remainder, lying forsaken in their cardboard beds, had already begun to wilt. We called a cab to take us to a member's home where we would spend the night, and the air in the cab was thick with the saccharine stench of withering gardenias. Somehow, we talked the cab driver into accepting the flowers as fare. As we stood on the sidewalk under the hazy glow of a streetlight, I remember his saying he would give them to his fiancée.

For one fleeting evening, I had succeeded in belonging, and as Emily Dickinson wrote, "Success is counted sweetest by those who ne'er succeed." I discovered on that moonlit night that belonging wasn't so sweet after all.

Storm Clouds

As the sky darkened, I left Grandmother Wood's house to walk toward home on Brickyard Hill. It was already late, and I wanted to get home before the imminent storm brought early darkness. At fifteen, I was not afraid to walk the approximate mile and a half. The decade of the '40s was a different time. People could saunter along Charleston streets, even late at night, without fear. The crime rate, always comparatively low in West Virginia, was not much of a problem then.

As I quickened my steps, I saw sheet lightning pulsing in dark clouds that rolled low over the distant hills. At last, I climbed the dirt bank leading to our house. Swirls of dust danced around me and spring-green leaves fluttered like frightened butterflies. As the wind whipped my hair about my face, I watched skinny tree limbs ride the wind earthward. Even the air itself had taken on an eerie yellow-gold cast. I ran the last few yards up the small bank leading home. As I ascended the concrete steps to our porch, large drops of rain splattered on the road, forming spider-like indentations. I dashed under the protection of the upper porch just as the heavens let loose.

My grandfather was rising from his wooden rocking chair and as he shoved it back out of the rain, one wide gray suspender drooped over his shoulder. He wore his usual outfit: faded black trousers of a once new suit and a yellowed dress shirt. Above the pounding of the rain, I could barely hear the rocker scrape against the concrete.

My grandfather looked out at the downpour and said, "You got home just in time. I'm 'fraid we're gonna have a real gully-washer this time. It's comin' from the West."

I looked toward the road but was unable to see anything beyond the gray wall of heavy rain. It blew horizontally all the way back to the outside wall of our house. A flash of lightning zigzagged toward earth. The electricity went off, and we rushed inside where my grandfather lit a couple of oil lamps. Darkness had arrived, and I watched giant shadows form on the walls as the lamplight flickered.

Lying awake much of that night, I listened to the continuing downpour. I had heard my grandparents say that if the rain didn't stop soon there would be floods. Early the next morning, the rains still came. Taffy-colored water gushed out of the hill and roared down the ditch alongside our house. Still, it rained hard all that day and into the next night.

The following morning, sun came through the kitchen window, painting large squares of light on the linoleum-covered floor. My mother and Aunt Ocie wanted to walk down into the valley to see whether anyone had been flooded. I remember descending the hill with them. I marveled at the beads of water glistening on leaves. The trees looked as if they had been studded with tiny diamonds; such is the view of youth. We crossed Washington Street and neared Two Mile Creek. It wasn't long before we could see that same frightening tan water. During the night, the floodwater had crept like a sneaky monster up the sides of houses where it destroyed everything many West Virginians had worked for all their lives.

Today, each time I drive my car past a service station near my home, I see two wreaths attached to a telephone pole. They were placed there in memory of loved ones lost to a recent flood. With the recurrence of spring floods each year, I am reminded that some things never change.

High School Graduation

June 1949 offered a major milestone in my life. Wearing a long white gown, I sat under warm lights on the stage at the Municipal Auditorium in Charleston, West Virginia. Sitting with more than 300 other graduates of the Stonewall Jackson High School class, I waited for my diploma. The boys wore dark suits. All the girls, except me, cradled in their arms a dozen long-stemmed red roses. I carried eleven. Perhaps by the time the florist filled my order, there were only eleven left. I don't remember the speaker or what was said, although I now know the speaker must have worked long hours on a talk that would soon be forgotten.

During those tender years, I admired the popular students. They were the ones who wore the latest fashions first, flashed confident smiles, belonged to several clubs, served as class presidents, and wrote for the school paper. They took college prep courses because they knew they were going to college. Their futures were bright. I took stenographic courses because I knew I was going to be a secretary. To have higher hopes would have been foolish. Anyway, I was contented to follow in my Aunt Phyllis's footsteps.

Now, when I look through my tattered red and gray *Jacksonian*, those same favored students smile at me from across the years, their faces still dewy-fresh with youth. Except for the few with whom I grew to adulthood, I lost track of my fellow classmates. For that reason, I didn't attend the reunions.

The years passed, and I lived a lifetime before finally deciding to reunite with those who had sat with me on a stage so many years earlier. I had been a secretary (a hard and stressful job regardless of the talent or lack thereof). Then I found myself a few years later hap-

Dolly Wood, the author, at the time of her high school graduation.

pily married with two children. I quit work and became a full-time mom, another stressful job for which there is no training. Being a new parent is like learning to swim by being thrown into the deep end of a pool. As a mother of small children, I tried returning to work and did serve on a governor's writing staff for a time, but our children needed me and I quit again. When our son and daughter entered junior high school, I entered college. Just before our son entered college, I received my first degree. And within two years, after graduate school, I was hired on a tenure track at a local college. I loved teaching from the first minute. I had found my niche even if it was late in life.

It was in 1989 that I decided to attend our fortieth class reunion. The invitation came on stylish gray stationery with red print. The print assured me that the committee members were keeping it simple, giving everyone a chance to reunite, to reminisce, and to catch up. Well, I thought I had a great deal to share. Here's what I discovered. Time had changed the faces, the figures, the hair. Time had broken hearts, had taken lives, and had destroyed health. Time, as the cliché goes, had leveled the playing field. I still admired my classmates, but for different reasons. They had learned to survive despite up-hill roads fate had forced them to climb. Some of the happiest students in high school held in late years only shattered fragments of dreams. Now I'm not writing a diary piece here. I'm writing to you graduates who might think your future couldn't be bright. Read my story and smile.

Since That First Journey

My first trip to Florida from West Virginia occurred in the summer of 1949, shortly after my graduation from Stonewall Jackson High School. Ray, my cousin, and his wife, Elda, had invited me to spend the summer with them in Miami. A husband and wife from Miami were visiting our neighbors and when they heard about my invitation, they said I could ride with them on their return trip.

On one misty morning, then, as sun burned away the fog, I packed my clothes in a small cardboard suitcase. I waited on our front porch for my ride. A short time later, I sat alone in the back seat of a car as the three of us headed south. It was not only my first trip to Florida, but it was also my first journey away from home. Having seen hills all my life, I was amazed when we passed miles of flat swampland on both sides of the narrow road. I had heard stories of travelers who had stopped their cars and walked back only a few feet into the swamps where they disappeared and were never heard from again. I knew that alligators, poisonous snakes, and other creatures remained hidden among the thick clumps of trees jutting out of the moss-green water, which was no more than three feet from the road. Despite the swamp's hidden dangers, it was a thing of fearsome beauty. I was drawn to its magnificence in the same way Ulysses was drawn to the sirens' songs.

I stayed in Miami the rest of that summer. I sunbathed in the backyard, enjoyed lunch at Burdine's with Elda and their two sons, Alan and Ronnie. In Ray and Elda's home, I ate real Italian spaghetti made from a recipe handed down in Elda's family. All things end, though, and too soon I boarded a Greyhound bus and rode back to West Virginia. Because I was a teenager who had never traveled alone, I was terrified to make that trip. Life is like that; we do many things because we have no choice. If I was to get back home, I had to make that trip alone.

My friend Barbara had moved away from Brickyard Hill, but her new home was still within walking distance from my house. Across the two-lane blacktop road from her house was Sovine's Soda Fountain where we teenagers could sit in a booth, sip Cokes, and dance to jukebox music. On my first return to Sovine's after my Florida trip, I wore an aqua sun-back dress, which highlighted the golden tan I had acquired in the Deep South. I'm sure the sun damaged my fair skin, but I gave that no thought. I showed off my tan and thought I was one pretty girl, sophisticated and well traveled.

Since that first journey, which in many ways was my initiation into adulthood, I've made countless trips to Miami and to Myrtle Beach. Up and down the East Coast, back and forth, my husband, Bill, and I traveled each summer for many years. We sometimes took his mom, dad, and brother. Motels back then were hit and miss. My father-in-law, Howard, and I always went in to check the room before we registered, for we were both finicky. If we saw a bug or the room smelled musty (that was often the case), we turned thumbs down and continued to look. My mom even moved to Miami, where she lived for years before returning home. After Bill and I had our son and daughter, we drove southward as a foursome. We passed Stuckey's, Howard Johnson motels, and gas stations with small mom-and-pop grocery stores behind the pumps. We passed water towers that looked like large oranges on tall green stems. We passed sideshows in which snakes and alligator wrestling drew large crowds. Each restaurant and motel was unique. We never knew what we were going to get, but traveling was an adventure. Today, we can zip from one state to another and wouldn't know which state we were in without the telltale green signs. Fast-food chains and motels are identical regardless of the location. Life is in the fast lane now, but I miss the individuality that was the America of yesteryear.

Night of Terror

A heavy summer rain had cleansed the earth the night before. As I walked down the hill to catch the city bus, I noticed beads of water still clinging to the foliage bordering the unpaved road. Everything smelled fresh, scrubbed of all impurities. Because dark clouds promised another storm that morning, I carried my umbrella, along with my purse and paper bag containing my office shoes, black high heels, each with closed toe and heel.

Our neighbors' rural mailboxes and ours were lined up at the foot of the hill. Whenever the steep road was muddy, I wore old penny loafers off the hill and after changing into my office shoes, I left the loafers in the back of our mailbox. I remember that day in the early '50s and with good reason.

After my workday at a local bank, I attended a law class sponsored by the American Institute of Banking. When I left the class that evening, drivers were already turning on their headlights. Rain had continued throughout the day, so darkness came early. I boarded the red city bus for my thirty-minute trip home. I sat in a front seat and looked at the raindrops clinging to the bus windows. As I was transported to the country, outside I saw only the blackness of night.

When I stepped down from the bus, I had to face oncoming traffic as I walked about a block to the foot of the hill where my penny loafers waited in our mailbox. Traffic was sparse, and only two cars passed me that evening, both shining their headlights on me like spotlights. The first car drove past and I turned to watch its red taillights disappear in the distance. The second car passed me, then made a U-turn across the road. Feeling uneasy, I looked to see it coming slowly toward me. I grabbed my loafers, hurriedly put them on, and began running up the hill.

I looked back once and saw that the car was parked at the foot of the hill and the two front doors of the car were open. The lights were still on and the engine was running. I saw two men leave the car and start walking rapidly up the hill. I knew where every large rock and pothole were located on that road, and I ran so fast that I don't remember my feet touching the ground.

I could hear each heavy footfall behind me, and once one of the men yelled, "Wait a minute." I knew they did not know my name, or they would have called it.

Only twenty years old, I was nonetheless gasping for breath by the time I reached the avenue where our house was located. Just as I started to run past our next-door neighbors' house, I heard Princess, their German shepherd, bark once. Then she did something she had been trained not to do. She jumped the tall chain-link fence around her yard and stopped in the middle of the road. Standing between my pursuers and me, she growled at the men, who turned and ran back down the hill. Wagging her tail, Princess came to me and stayed with me until I entered the door of my house.

When my family wanted to know what was wrong, I couldn't speak. I had heard the expression *scared speechless*, but that was the first time I knew the reality of it.

Later, sitting on our front porch, I could feel the dampness from the recent rain, but I no longer felt that it had washed all impurities from the earth.

Uncle Jack

Sitting on a backless bench of weathered wood, Uncle Jack leaned against the cool stucco of our house. At the edge of the front porch, morning glory vines boasting lavender-blue flowers climbed on twine up past the banister to the overhead porch where my grandfather had anchored each strand of heavy string. The vines filtered the morning sun so that light and shadow danced in ever-changing patterns like colors in a rotating kaleidoscope.

Even during the sweltering dog days of the early '40s, when others donned cool clothes, our visitor wore a seedy black suit and a broad-brimmed hat the color of an ancient raven, a hat he never removed during his visits. His white shirt, unbuttoned at the neck, hinted at his only concession to the stifling weather. Uncle Jack smoked a pipe with a stem that dipped and swirled into a graceful curve just as it reached the bowl. His face, clean-shaven, revealed deep-set eyes of faded brown, bushy gray eyebrows, a large nose, and a jutting chin, which my grandfather called stubborn. He was of blood kin to neither anyone in my family nor to anyone in our vicinity. Like Uncle Sam, he needed no last name, for everyone in the small corner of my childhood world knew him only as Uncle Jack.

Our front porch, like a stage on which countless dramas played themselves out, provided the place where I received much of my education and amusement when

I was a young girl without siblings. It was there that I listened to adult conversations, observed distinctive mannerisms, and sensed raw emotions. It was there that I listened to the exchange of tall tales and real-life stories. It was there that I learned the art of discourse.

Uncle Jack and my grandfather held long, and sometimes heated, conversations. While one was a yellow-dog Democrat, the other was a red-hot Republican. Their debates were like morality plays, with good and evil being decided by each viewer's political preference. I can still see Uncle Jack jabbing his curve-stemmed pipe straight into the air as if doing so blasted home his points. My grandfather, cheeks flaming red, reinforced his arguments by pounding the concrete porch with the tip of his cane, a cane that had been fashioned from a small tree limb. The two old men argued back and forth for hours, but they nonetheless remained friends. It was a time when face-to-face discussions were a form of entertainment and enlightenment. During each of Uncle Jack's visits, after the pair had set each other straight in political matters, they moved on to a discussion of World War II, a discussion that healed any superficial wounds previously incurred from their political wrangling. When talk of war surfaced, they were Americans first, of one mind, united.

I knew when each visit was about to end. Our guest would get a mischievous twinkle in his eyes, glance my way, then look straight at my grandfather and begin speaking pig Latin. Like comic relief in a Shakespearean play, jokes—sometimes a bit off-color—ended Uncle Jack's sojourn on our front porch. After chuckling at his own jokes—he did that and no one minded—he rose from the weathered bench, stretched his arms overhead, and removed the pipe from his mouth. He bent over the banister on which he lightly tapped his pipe upside down to remove any leftover ashes. Then hobbling to the edge of the porch, he walked sideways like a crab down the three concrete steps leading to the dusty road in front of our house. He threw up his hand in a farewell gesture and disappeared as he walked slowly over the hill. Another typical Sunday afternoon had ended.

We had no e-mail, voice mail, cell phones, telephones pagers, or palm-held computers. Still, during that summer evening, when the sun glowed like a stage light as it coated our porch in transparent gold, we had enjoyed the art of genuine communication.

Door-to-Door Sales

After many years, I can still see her. With salt-and-pepper hair twisted in a tight bun at the crown of her head, she had a couple of tendrils, slightly wavy, that hung loosely on either side of her face. Thin to the point of looking emaciated, she nonetheless demonstrated vigorous strength. My mom called her wiry. She was.

Climbing our hill on any given summer day when the air was sticky with humidity, she lugged a large black satchel made of canvas. It bulged with catalogs and advertisements of the latest Maisonette Frocks. Miss Morris was a saleslady who was proud of her wares, which consisted of dresses for women and children. There were no jeans or slacks featured in her catalogs—just dresses. In fact, Miss Morris wore only dresses. Flat-heeled shoes and hose completed each of her outfits.

By the time she arrived on our front porch, she was ready for a glass of ice-cold well water and for a bit of neighborhood gossip. Sometimes she ate her lunch, which she told us was always the same, a single candy bar. She sat for a while, then retrieved a heavy catalog from her satchel and passed it over to one of my aunts or my mother. They took turns browsing while Miss Morris got out small metal-framed eyeglasses, which she perched on the end of her nose. When she looked out and above her glasses, her pale blue eyes sparkled with anticipation of a sale. But visiting was as important to her as a sale.

At other times, sales reps from various companies called on us. I remember a salesman from a company that sold sterling silverware. I don't remember the name of the company, but he convinced me that it was high time I buy something for my hope chest. Hope chests were still popular, for the end-all in most young girls' lives in the '40s and '50s was to marry. So I purchased a starter set of Lady Hilton pattern solid sterling silverware. A few weeks later, the salesman brought my silver in a mahogany box lined with green felt. I paid a little on it each month until the final payment was made. I still have a few tarnished pieces in the back of a cabinet drawer.

The Fuller brush salesman and a coffee salesman also paid visits to our house. Selling and buying offered opportunities for human contact, for conversation, for catching up on the world beyond our neighborhood.

Today, we can sit in front of our computers and order everything from bikes to books. If we don't like ordering online, we can go to a large chain store and search for merchandise. Finding what we want to buy in most stores today is easier than finding a salesperson to help us. The small hardware stores are fast disappearing. Barbershops where men can exchange the day's gossip are becoming increasingly rare.

When we heard that a car had struck Miss Morris as she stepped off a red city bus, that she had been killed, we were saddened by the loss of a close friend. Her death has since become a symbol to me of the end of a time that will never return. With every gain there is loss. We now enjoy conveniences we would not want to give up, but the cost has been less human contact, fewer face-to-face conversations on shady front porches.

A Love Story

When the Reverend Willard Carney was young and beginning his ministry, he frequently stopped by our house on Sundays. He usually arrived about mid-morning when shade still cooled the front porch. During each visit, he and my grandfather chatted as my mother and grandmother prepared the Sunday dinner in the back of the kitchen. Following dinner, the men returned to the front porch and talked until church time.

Like most West Virginians in the '40s, Willard was not wealthy. He never owned a large house or drove a new car, but those would not have been important to him anyway. His entire life was devoted to his calling, and he gave unselfishly of himself. In retrospect, I know he sacrificed much in his own life to serve others.

After each Sunday visit, the preacher and various family members (depending on who was living in the house at the time) walked out the dirt road to the church where Willard Carney delivered his sermon. My mother told me that my Uncle Hobert Frame deeded land to Willard's church. To this day that land is still church property, now serving as the church parking lot. Throughout the ensuing years, Willard would deliver countless sermons at what was then called Prayer and Faith Tabernacle.

As time passed, Willard's life—like most lives—was punctuated by death and love and births. Each time that illness and death visited our family he was there. He preached five funerals for members of my family. Despite his giving of self to others, Willard had a personal life that was filled with love.

Mary Marcum, when only eleven years old, saw him for the first time. She was in the back seat of a Model T Ford, and he was standing on a street corner. Despite her age, she said it was love at first sight. Looking at him, she knew that handsome man would be hers one day. This was surely puppy love, for he was fourteen years older than Mary. It proved to be much more. Mary and Willard were married when she was eighteen and he was thirty-two. They had five children: Faith, Hope, Charity, Angel, and "Bill."

Mary said that Willard had been quite ill himself before his death, but he continued to preach. Then one day, he told his congregation he was ready to leave this world and hoped he would die behind the pulpit. Two weeks later, in the middle of a sermon, he had a fatal heart attack. A gentle gentleman who wept unashamedly when others suffered, he spent his entire adult life as a good Samaritan. I can still see him sitting around our old table or enjoying conversations in the shade of our front porch on Brickyard Hill.

Homes of the Heart

No matter how many people have bought and inhabited the house where I grew to adulthood, the stucco house in my mind still belongs to my grandparents, although they have been dead for many years. I have dis-

Back row: Margaret Gillispie, Rosie Gillispie, Georgie Vogel, Lois Taylor. Middle row: Barbara Gillispie, Melvin Gillispie, David Gillispie, Erma Vogel. Front row: Doris Mooney, Dolly Wood (author).

covered that we can go home again, but each time we pay an emotional price.

It is a bright summer day as I drive past the old house. Its upper porch floor is decaying, for the run-down structure has been neglected. My grandparents' home, my home, is now a government-owned house and is rented to low-income persons. I note that whoever lives in our house is nonetheless working hard to transform it into their home. Two calico cats sleep contentedly on the lower concrete porch. They are partially hidden by four clay pots filled with red geraniums. The yard to the right side of the house as I face it once had a retaining wall that held back a sloping bank where my grandmother's flowers bloomed. The lower part of the yard was level.

I have an old photograph in which my childhood friends and I are in that yard. My Aunt Sissy had baked a cake with my name on it. We are gathered around a small green table on which my birthday cake holds seven candles. I aim a toothless grin at the camera as if I'll never grow old.

Years later, as I drive past the old house, I see that the retaining wall is gone and the yard slopes all the way to the blacktop road in front. I remember my youth and a lump catches in my throat.

I have had other homes of course. When in 1956, my husband and I passed a small cottage with a for-sale sign, we called to ask the price. The total cost was $7,500, and it was owner-financed. We didn't even have to make a down payment. We painted the cottage a dark green with white trim and added a bedroom and bath to the back. That house still holds a special place in our hearts, for both our son and daughter were born when we lived there. To this day, when we drive past "our little green house," we feel that it's still ours, although strangers live there and even use the curving stone walk that my husband built. The light post he installed at the end of the walk is still there, lighting the way for strangers who live in our house.

Life's journey took us from there to a subdivision called Brookhaven, and from there we traveled to Louisiana, where my husband continued to work for Union

Carbide. We purchased a large four-bedroom house. It was never home, though, for we knew our stay was temporary. Returning to West Virginia, we purchased a house on the banks of the Kanawha River and from there, we went to a townhouse. None of these places felt like home.

After many years, I have come full circle. We live in a house that we totally renovated. The original structure, though, was built by my Uncle Hobert, the same uncle who had helped to build the house on Brickyard Hill. The structure looked like a miniature version of my childhood home. Made of stucco, it had the same symmetry with a center door and flanking windows, all topped by a hip roof. We have lived in our Goldtown house for almost ten years. I am home at last.

The Appointment

On the day I was to pick up my uncle for a doctor's appointment, many years had passed since I had left my childhood home. The morning of the appointment was warm for early autumn, and the sun's incandescent glow bathed the countryside. I parked my brown Thunderbird in front of a small one-room building and a few minutes later stood at the door of the structure. I hesitated before knocking, as if my hesitation could somehow make the dreaded doctor's visit disappear. The air was heavy with the odor of damp earth from the previous night's rain and the fragrance of old-fashioned white roses. In wet clusters, they hung on a nearby bush, bending the branches toward the ground that was already carpeted with wilting petals. At the top of the bank to my right, I saw a white bungalow. Beside the house was a clothesline from which hung khaki work pants, matching shirts, and blue bed sheets printed with tiny pink flowers. I had not met the elderly couple who had welcomed my uncle onto their land, but he had spoken kindly of them.

I knocked lightly on the door, which was already slightly ajar. Stepping inside, I saw my Uncle Alfred sitting at a rectangular table. He wore dark dress pants, dark socks and shoes, but he wore no shirt. He was so thin that I could see the outline of each rib. He was shaving and had propped a square mirror in front of a Quaker's Oats box. As he contorted his face for a closer shave, he said, "I'll be ready in a minute." I told him I would wait for him in the car, knowing he would not rush. He was an easy-going man who had never rushed in his life, regardless of the circumstances.

About an hour later, as I absently leafed through outdated magazines in the doctor's waiting room, a nurse's voice interrupted my thoughts. She asked me to follow her, and we walked down the hall to the doctor's office. I saw my uncle sitting in a chair in front of a large cherry desk. The doctor offered me a seat and the three of us faced one another in silence for a few uncomfortable moments. Looking down at a paper clip he was flipping over and over, the physician cleared his throat and said, "I was just telling Mr. Frame that he has lung cancer and must be hospitalized at once. My nurse is making the arrangements."

Uncle Alfred was admitted to a hospital where I visited him routinely during the next two months. At first, the prognosis looked bright. We were told that the cancer was confined to one lung and that lung could be removed. We waited expectantly for the surgery to be scheduled. One day, I listened to my uncle tell a visitor that things were not as bad as he had first thought, that the doctors were going to remove one lung. He would be all right.

My uncle had no health insurance, and the operation never occurred. During one visit, I was told that the doctors would not do anything extraordinary "when the time came." The prognosis now was certain death. I watched as my mom's brother grew weaker each day. The last time I visited him, he told me that he had been given a shower and had been painfully scrubbed and almost scalded. I could see no evidence of scalding and assumed that the medication had made him delusional. However, the next day he died and was taken to a funeral home. His comments about the shower still haunt me.

My uncle was buried on a bleak day in January 1974. A basket of roses at the foot of his casket reminded me of my visit to his one-room home where the scent of white roses intermingled with the damp earth. Three members of my family have been claimed by killer cancer. Today, it continues to kill, but an increasing number of cancer sufferers are living beyond that magical five-year period. There is hope.

One Misty Morning

One early morning, as heavy fog obscured the pine trees at the edge of our yard, my husband went into the garage, approached his workbench, and there it was, lying right in the middle of the table as if it had simply dropped from the ceiling. Yellowed with age, a small envelope still displayed a two-cent postage stamp in the upper right-hand corner. In the center of the faded red stamp, an oval frame held the side profile of George

Washington. Postmarked March 24, 1925, 5 P.M., the envelope was addressed to my late uncle at only "Station B, Charleston, W. Va."

The address and enclosed letter were written in a time before abbreviations of states were changed to accommodate technology in post offices, before zip codes, before computers, and long before e-mail and virtual mailboxes. Written in an era when communication often took the form of hand-written letters, the missive revealed language with a haunting rhythm; it revealed poetry within prose.

"This beautiful evening affords me time and pleasure to try and answer your card received this morning."

These quoted words provide the introduction of the letter that had been written on a single sheet of lined notebook paper. The page, now almost a century old, is so fragile that it is torn at the fold. My uncle is warned to tear the letter up and burn it because the writer wants his message to remain a secret between sender and receiver. Here I am, almost a century later, reading about the lives of two young men and others, all of whom are long gone. Doing so gives me a strange perspective on life and the changes that have taken place during the past three-quarters of a century.

The author signs only his first name, so no one now living would be able to identify him. He says in his letter that my uncle has a "funny side," which surprises me because I remember my Uncle Alfred only as a middle-aged man and later as an old man who never revealed to me his sense of humor.

When I consider the writing style of the ancient message, though, I know we've lost something of great value. I recognize the care the writer has given to each word, to each sentence, and because of that, I feel the warmth and sincerity of the author. Reading the letter, I witness genuine and original communication from one human being to another.

Today, we have writing tools at our disposal that would astonish these two friends who exchanged their thoughts by painstakingly writing word after word, and carrying the message to the post office, then waiting patiently for a reply.

On a computer, we can delete entire paragraphs at the stroke of a single key. We can rearrange whole sections. With ease, we can copy and paste and send entire documents, yet we've lost something in the throes of technology. Daily, I receive canned e-mails that the senders have not written. Some forwarded messages tell me that I'll have bad luck if I don't, in turn, forward these e-mails to others who must also forward them lest they have bad luck. One canned message told me if I would send the e-mail to five more persons, my phone would ring within five minutes. If I would send the message to ten additional persons after that, I would have good luck for one year. These canned e-mails often prevent carefully written exchanges between friends. They provide obstacles to the kind of original communication my husband found in the middle of a workbench during one misty morning.

Far from Brickyard Hill

Sitting in the Governor's Mansion in Charleston, West Virginia, I watched a woman with blue-white hair. She sat across the aisle in one of the small folding chairs that formed rows on both sides of the room. The chairs were jammed so tightly that we in the audience felt like

one entity. It was as if our shoulders were welded together. An author stood behind a lectern and read ex-
cerpts from her novel. As the novelist read, I noticed
the white-haired woman in the royal blue suit wore diamonds that glittered under overhead lights. She had a
problem though. The lady couldn't stay awake and as
she dozed, she leaned increasingly toward the aisle. I
held my breath as she leaned farther and farther toward
the floor. The man beside her didn't know what to do
except shrug and smile nervously. Finally, he gently
nudged her, and she awoke, trying to regain her com-
posure. Soon, she began to nod off again. This time she
laid her head on the stranger's shoulder and slept
throughout the remainder of the program.

At the same reading, another woman walked up and
down the aisles before the event began. She wanted
everyone to see that she was there attending a cultural
happening. Honestly, you can sense when someone is
doing that, which is why I try not to be so obvious. I
resort only to sitting a little taller in my chair.

Before the author or performer made an appearance
at each gathering, the VIPs began to enter. They didn't
have to arrive early to get seats, as the rest of us had to
do. At each performance, the important people had reserved seats in front that were separated from our tiny
chairs by a velvet rope. Since the governor was sympa-
thetic to the working person, I had my own reservations about his reservations for the elite. No doubt I
would have felt better about it all had I been one of the
elite.

At one of these auspicious affairs, I was able to see
Carl Sagan, although I couldn't hear him. In a creative
effort to make the surroundings resemble the universe,
the first lady had chairs set up on the second floor of
the Capitol Building around the rotunda. Because of the

domed cavity overhead, I thought it was a clever idea, but when Sagan began talking, his voice echoed from speaker to speaker. So, so, so, that, that, that the whole event turned into a kind of tragicomedy. I bet someone caught it over that little show.

Another time, I listened to Jim Lehrer. He did a fine rendition of the last train call before the final passenger boarded a train in yesteryear. Another time, I was able to hear a famous jazz band. At all events, though, I enjoyed most of all watching people play pretend games. Let's pretend we love cultural events. Let's pretend that highbrow novels are always deep instead of sometimes boring. Let's pretend we know more than we know. Shucks, I love those games, too. Each time, I sat in a tiny chair at the Governor's Mansion, though, I was reminded of how far I had traveled beyond Brickyard Hill, where we children knew when we were playing games.

D-Con for That Morning Smile

When one is ninety-one years old, one sits in a doctor's office on a regular basis. As my mother frequents various doctors' offices, I accompany her. Speaking of regular, though, my mother is obsessed with, well, regularity, all of which has brought me to a surprising conclusion. I've noticed that there are two times in life when people are obsessed with regularity. The first time is when parents have a newborn. They begin to dwell on the baby's bodily functions and will discuss every detail even when dining with childless friends in a restaurant. The parents' remarks leave the friends aghast as their eyes widen and mouths gape open. Young parents see nothing amiss in discussing a topic that, before the child's birth (when they were perhaps still newly-weds), they would have never mentioned, even to each other. The second time in life that regularity takes center stage is when old age arrives in earnest. The end-all of the day, the one event about which the old person focuses, is—okay here it is again—regularity. I'm trying to be as ladylike as possible while discussing an indelicate subject. Before parents have a newborn and after the newborn is grown, they remain embarrassed at the mere mention of any kind of bodily function except a few, such as eating, sleeping, and yawning. Even burping or its mention draws howls from teenagers and scowls from young and middle-aged adults.

Advertisers are well aware of old folks' needs. Television commercials that interrupt the evening news almost as often as we blink our eyes tout products that interest old viewers because old viewers (euphemistically called senior citizens) are the ones who regularly (no pun intended) watch the news. In one commercial, a woman driving a school bus is grouchy because . . . well, you know why. After taking the advertised product, she finds that her life has completely turned around. She's nothing but sweetness and smiles the next morning.

Now, back to the visit to the doctor. Sitting beside me amid lined-up chairs and outdated magazines, my mother leaned close to me and said, "Dolly, don't forget to get me some D-Con at the drugstore."

"Mom, why do you need D-Con?"

"Well, my land, we talked about it not fifteen minutes ago. Don't you remember?"

"Oh, you mean FiberCon®." Of course, I remembered. How could I forget?

Laughing at her own malapropism, she said, "I think my doctor got a real keek out of the stories he read about me."

"Oh, yes, I think so, too," said I.

The doctor had bought a copy of my *More than Penny Candy* and told my mother that he had laughed and cried all the way through the book. My mom was sure he was referring to the essays about her, but she didn't know whether he laughed or cried when reading "her" stories.

At any rate, my mother's conclusion now is this: If you want to start each day with a smile (like that TV lady driving the school bus), don't forget your D-Con.

Bim's Boys and Other Motherisms

"I haven't heard a thing from Bim's boys in a long time. Have you heard anything from them?"

It was my mother's voice coming from the back seat of our car as my husband drove over the interstate. In the passenger seat, I turned around with a knowing smile. This was going to be fun. Mom's comment and question were aimed at my mother-in-law who sat beside Mom.

With a puzzled expression, similar to the kind a cartoonist draws of someone totally bewildered by a nonsensical comment, my mother-in-law said, "Esther, I don't believe I know Bim, so I'm sure I don't know his boys."

"Oh, yes you do, Ora. You know Bim Crosby, the singer. Everybody knows Bim. His boys are almost as famous as he is."

"Oh, you mean Bing Crosby," said Ora with that surprised look of enlightenment we're sometimes privileged to see.

"Whatever."

The "whatever" ended the conversation about Bim and his boys.

A few years later, Mom was talking to me about a local celebrity whose pregnancy had been charted on a television station. She looked at me with great concern in her brown eyes. "You know I heard they're going to introduce pain to Natalie."

"Mom, what are you talking about?" asked I, as I imagined a young damsel named Natalie tied to a chair in an abandoned farmhouse.

"My land, Dolly, don't you watch the news? You know Natalie on television. They're going to introduce pain."

"Oh, you mean that they're going to induce labor?" said I.

"Whatever."

Thus, another conversation ended with Mom's, er, closure, her period at the end of a paragraph, her "whatever."

Another time, she was talking about a woman who comes to her apartment to help her with chores and the like. My mother called me and said, "Mary rubbed lotion on my back this morning. It felt so good that I thought I was getting a corsage."

"Mom, do you mean massage?"

"Whatever."

I've been interpreting my mom's words for other listeners for as long as I can remember. In the middle of one night when she was staying with us, she yelled, "Dolly, my year's bleeding."

I rushed to her bedside and her year surely was bleeding. My husband and I rushed her to the closest hospital. The doctor who treated my mom spoke English only as a second language. You can see the scene now. There was my mom with her special dialect. There was the doctor speaking broken English, and there was I to interpret, just as the police officer did on *Sanford and Son.*

The doctor asked, "Have you been putting something shop in your eah?"

She appeared mystified. I interpreted. "Mom, have you been putting something sharp in your ear?

She eyed the doctor suspiciously and said, "My year eetched."

The poor doctor was at his wit's end, but again I came to the rescue. "Her ear itched."

He proceeded to tell her that she should never put anything sharp in her ears, but she had no idea what he said and, in fact, had lost interest anyway. She was busy watching men in orange jumpsuits. On the back of each was written, "[Local] County Jail." I don't know which was more difficult for doctors to treat in the middle of that foggy night, my mom with her speech patterns or the inmates with their behavioral patterns. Anyway, since that night many years ago, I haven't heard a thing from Bim's boys. Have you?

Stories from the Exit Ramp

Death continues to blow its numbing breath across my heart. Growing weaker each day from a failing heart, my mom drew her last breath at 12:25 p.m. on February 11, 2003. My daughter and I were at her bedside, along with several of the wonderful employees at Eldercare in Ripley, West Virginia. I discovered as I held her hand that there is a difference of a zillion light years between life and death, even though at the end of each person's life they share the same split second.

People have wondered how my mom felt about my essays focusing on her and her dialect. She loved them. In fact, as I sat with her in a doctor's office one day in late summer, she said, "I think your readers get a real keek out of my stories."

Shortly after she entered Eldercare, the staff members who cared for her began to go into her room when they had a few extra minutes. They liked to hear her talk and to listen to her quick comebacks. Some said she was witty; others called her spunky. She had lost weight, so she weighed only about a hundred pounds, and she was five feet, seven inches tall. Even when she became so weak she could no longer get out of bed, she called the shots. If she didn't want to take her medicine, she didn't. Sometimes, she told me stories about how she was treated (and I knew she was treated well). I watched as workers came in and kissed her on the forehead before they went home.

One day, Mother said, "Dolly, one of the workers here is calling me a rat."

"Oh, Mom, you're imagining things. Surely not," said I.

About that time, Marcie entered the room and said to my mom, "Okay, little Rugrat, let's get you dressed."

A short time later, Mom began calling Marcie "Tree Frog," a nickname that the other employees picked up. Tree Frog will make an excellent nurse one day.

Another time, Mom told our son that I thought she was crazy because she had seen a little man crawl across the ceiling. She added, "But I saw him before I went crazy."

What does one say to a Gracie Allen line like that? Her dehydration had caused her to become disoriented and generally confused at times, but eventually the little man disappeared, and she was as sharp as ever (most of the time).

Nature has a way of hiding reality from patients who look pitiful to visitors. My mom must have believed herself to be still young and beautiful, although we saw an old woman whose face revealed the closeness of death. She believed that a young man who cared for her at Eldercare was in love with her. Chris was one of the most compassionate workers I've known and had a way with the residents. He, too, will make an outstanding nurse one day. I think he did love Mom just as he loved all the residents at Eldercare, but that's different from being in love. Then, there was the minister who came to the nursing home almost every single day. He delivered sermons and sang to the congregation in the dining room. Mostly, though, he visited the residents who were unable to leave their rooms. The Reverend Darrell Tackett gives of himself and his time. He has genuine love for old people who have lived long lives and are often left abandoned with no one to visit them. My mother thought there was no one better than Darrell Tackett or, get this, no one better looking. She began to watch for him each day, just as she watched for me. I met Darrell's wife, whom I found to be as caring as her husband. Darrell led the final service for my mom. She would have liked that.

In Search of Lost Worlds

My mother told me she was born in a log house near Two Mile Creek. Like a person about whom I read years ago in Ripley's syndicated newspaper column, "Believe It or Not," my mother was born in the last month of the year, on the last day of the month, in the last hour of the day, and in the last minute of the hour. She had two sisters and three brothers. She was the last born in her family.

I've wondered about my mom's life before I was part of it, just as my son and daughter must wonder about my world and their father's before they were born. There is a world forever lost to each of us, a world about which we know little. Still, each hidden world has helped to weave the fabric of our character. Knowing something of our parents' early life helps us to better understand them and ourselves as individuals.

During conversations, Mom gave me glimpses into her childhood. These are the few things she told me, and they are probably part fiction because memory is half selection and half creation.

She said that when she was a tiny girl she had a recurring dream. Casting a gloomy light, a burning oil lamp was left in her room each night. As the flame quivered and flickered, it threw scary shadows that moved in ever-changing shapes on the log walls.

Mom said, "After I'd go to sleep, I dreamed that the devil came into my room and blew out the light. I'd wake up, scream, and jump out of bed. I'd run to Mommy and Poppy's room and leap into their bed."

I wasn't sure when my mother quit going to school. One time, she said she went through the fourth grade; another time it was only the second. She hated school because by the time her parents let her attend, she was already nine years old and taller than all the children in her class. When rains came and a nearby creek flooded, she was not allowed to walk across the footbridge. Besides, she said school gave her a headache. She ultimately taught herself to read and write and signed her first name, Esther, with flair.

With no marketable skills, she spent a lifetime in menial jobs. She met and married my father, Paul Wood, when she was only eighteen years old, and I was born when she was nineteen. She left my dad for the last time when I was about five. She worked at the Elite Laundry in Charleston at one time. When I married, she moved to Miami, Florida, where she met her second husband. After his death, she returned to Charleston. Her nightmares returned when she was in her seventies, and often she would dive or jump out of bed, but there were no parents to comfort her.

When Mom was ninety-two, she lay helpless in her bed at Eldercare. Her bedside lamp gave a subtle light but cast no dark shadows. It should have, for the ultimate nightmare for me occurred when she died. Just as she was the last to be born in a family of six, she was the last to die. I'll never know more about her childhood that helped make her who she was, and, in turn, helped to mold me.

Esther Wood Cassinet, the author's mother.

REFLECTIONS

Over the Rainbow

It is spring as I gaze at the night sky. Invisible to us during the day, with the coming of darkness, the stars have made their appearance. They are scattered throughout the blue-black firmament, appearing to me only as tiny shimmering lights as far as I can see. Standing in our front yard, I turn around and around and look in all directions at the domed ceiling overhead. Would scientists ever call what I see a miracle, something beyond their comprehension? I watch the heavens with the wide-eyed wonder of a child, for I am no astronomer.

Scientists have named, I believe, eighty-eight constellations. Each forms an arbitrary sketch, a picture, if we draw an imaginary line from star to star in any one of the known clusters. If I stretch imaginary lines from star to star in the Orion constellation, I am supposed to see the image of the giant hunter (Orion) who pursued Pleiades and was killed by Artemis. My imagination fails me, though, because I see only a jumble of stars. I suppose the whole effort with Orion is somewhat like watching clouds and seeing different shapes—each shape, depending on each viewer's perception. Still, some pictures are obvious even without the lines. I can see clearly the Big Dipper in the constellation Ursa Major. If I look in another direction, I can view what I think is Pleiades, named after the seven daughters of Atlas in Greek mythology. I can see only six stars in this cluster, but astronomers tell us hundreds are hiding from view.

I wonder what else is hiding from our limited vision. It seems to me that with each new scientific discovery, the experts are faced with even more mysteries, more questions. Often, what was believed to be true in the past becomes fiction in the present. Fact and fiction blur like colors in the rainbow. At one time, the earth was proclaimed to be the center of the universe by those who study these marvels. Then it was the sun. What is it today? I wonder.

Here's the thing. Despite all the naming and locating and line-drawing and intense studying of heavenly objects, no one—not the most erudite of all humans—can tell me what lies beyond those stars, what lies over the edge of the universe, what lies beyond the rainbow. You see; we think in terms of boundaries, of limits. So here I am on this spring night looking at an infinite universe with my small finite mind. All this presents a human dilemma—a puzzle I cannot solve, a puzzle no one can solve.

The English Romantic poet, William Blake, knew we could not really hold infinity in the palms of our hands or eternity in an hour. Of course, we cannot, so his poem will have to suffice. Although beautiful, his poetry cannot compare to the expanse of heavens. We cannot even imagine infinity—something without beginning or end, something that has always been and will always be, something that stretches away forever, something that has no boundaries. We can talk about infinity. We can utter the word *eternity*. We can even pretend to know more than we know, for the human ego comes as close to something without boundaries as anything I know. Still, on this spring night as I gaze at the stars glimmering against a black velvet backdrop, I know how little I know.

Lady in the Argyle Socks

Wearing white canvas shoes with pink and gray argyle socks that stopped just below her knees, she sat on the front row of my college literature class. Sometimes, she wore white slacks; other times, she wore walking shorts. Always, though, she wore those argyle socks. A knit top or sweater usually completed her outfit. With shiny rimless glasses, pale yellow hair (colored to hide the gray) and bright red fingernails, she was petite and, in her own way, chic. Folks who had known her for many years claimed she was at least seventy-five, and they always added, "if she's a day." She would never discuss her age, believing it was no one's business, and she was right. Further rumors claimed she was wealthy. She had audited my introductory class so that no grade would be involved. Anyway, she had long since run her career race, so college credits were meaningless to her.

During the beginning of the semester, we covered the short story. Then, we moved to poetry, always the students' least favorite genre. At first, they complained about the obscure language of many poems. They grumbled and said they couldn't grasp the meanings. I discussed the irony in some lines, the figurative language in others, and alliteration in still others. I talked about unreliable speakers and explained enjambment. I read poems aloud (the best way). Each year, most of the students eventually began to enjoy the works of the great poets. One time, a young man whispered to me that he was beginning to like "it" (he wouldn't say the word *poetry*), and I told him I wouldn't tell anyone if he wouldn't. He seemed relieved. But enticing students into the world of meter and rhythm took time, occasionally more time than one semester allowed.

My introductory literature class with the lady in the

argyle socks was held only one evening a week, and it therefore lasted almost three hours. During our break, the lady stood in the hall just outside the classroom door where, surrounded by young students, she held court. As they listened to every word, she recited lines from Shakespearean plays, poetry by the New England poets, and other poems she especially liked. Her ability to repeat words from memory astounded her listeners, for most of them had been taught that the memorization of anything by boring repetition was contrary to real learning. Still, I sensed their envy of this woman's talent.

At the end of one session, I asked the lady if she would mind standing in front of the room and reciting a few short poems or some lines from Shakespeare. I think she was delighted, for she said with a bright smile that she would choose something for the following week.

I let her use the first fifteen minutes or so of the next class period, and she used them well. Standing by the oak desk in front of the room and without benefit of a single note, she began speaking the opening lines of a famous poem by Dylan Thomas.

She said, "Do not go gentle into that good night/ Old age should burn and rave at close of day."

As we later discussed the poem and how the poet's father was near death at the time Thomas wrote those lines, I discovered that several students had figured out that "good night" meant death itself.

On a golden autumn day, years later, I heard that the student who had committed to memory a storehouse of literature had died. I was saddened and sensed a great loss. I'll never forget, though, how her own light burned brightly, illuminating a college classroom. During one semester, a long time ago, the lady in the argyle socks helped me to lure students into the magical world of words, poetic words.

A Time to Remember

Driving up a blacktop road toward home one cold spring evening, I noticed something lying still by the side of the road. As I drove closer, I saw that it was a small fawn. A car had apparently struck the deer. That a life had been snuffed out so early was especially sad to me because just as I stopped my car the fawn's mother bounded down the bank to my right and bolted across the road, running directly in front of my car. She came to an abrupt halt when she was beside her fawn. Then, she stood looking down in disbelief at her offspring. Even when I began to drive past her, she would not move. In my rearview mirror, I saw her nudging her fawn's head. In death's grip, it could not move.

I was reminded of a short story by Jesse Stuart. In the story, a young boy's father kills a large black snake on the family farm. The next morning, the boy finds a live black snake lying beside its dead mate. It seems clear, then, that we humans are not the only ones who remember loved ones lost to death. We are unique, though, in that we have set aside a national holiday for remembering our dead. The fact that we attend ceremonies and visit graves to leave flowers sets us apart from animals.

When I was a child, we never had cookouts on what was then called Decoration Day. Regardless of the day of the week, May 30 was the day we collectively honored our country's fallen heroes and our deceased family members. A few days before May 30, we gathered our few garden tools, freshly cut roses, canning jars, and a gallon of water. Then, we walked out a dusty road and through a narrow path bordered by tall weeds. At the end of the path, we entered Sattes Cemetery where we greeted both neighbors and strangers. Everyone worked hard cutting and raking weeds, but there was always time to visit. After we cleaned the graves and placed roses on each of two graves where my maternal aunts reposed, we walked back out the dusty road toward home. Four empty grave plots remained in our square of land in a cemetery that comprised only four acres. Despite the cemetery's modest size, a section was set aside to be used as a potter's field, a place where unknown or indigent persons were buried.

When we decorated those graves so many years ago, I had no idea that it was during the Civil War that Memorial Day had its beginnings. Women from the South began decorating graves of both Confederate and Union soldiers. Just as our Statue of Liberty has French ties, our Memorial Day probably does as well. A Southern woman with French blood suggested that May 30 be the day set aside for decorating graves because that was the day commemorating the return of Napoleon's remains to France. On May 5, 1868, General John Logan declared May 30 to be observed as a national day of remembering, and Decoration Day was first observed on May 30, of that same year. Today, to obtain a three-day weekend, we now celebrate Memorial Day on the last Monday in May.

Not only has the date of this holiday changed, but also our focus has changed. I remember when we first began to work on the house in which we now live. Each Memorial Day, we brought picnic supplies and had a cookout. That was only a few short years ago, and already that celebration has changed yet again for our family. My mother-in-law and father-in-law were always with us during those Memorial Day picnics. Now, they repose in Dunbar Cemetery, and all our holidays have been altered because of their absence. They, too, have become part of our loving memories, just as we, in time, will be but memories to our descendants. That cannot be altered no matter how much we wish it were otherwise.

I remember that dismal spring day when the mother deer mourned her loss. Later, as I daily passed by the dead deer, I noticed that someone had covered it with lime. For many weeks, I saw only a white blob as I passed. Then, one day, the deer had disappeared altogether, leaving only memories.

At the Seashore

Providing me with a catbird's seat for sea viewing, a high vinyl stool is one of four around a large table. Inside the screened balcony, I watch the long lines of white foam roll upon the beach and watch them return to the depths of the ocean. I listen to the rhythmic roar of waves as they beat against the sand, then move quickly out again. The tireless ocean never pauses in its cyclic movements.

Time advances as relentlessly as the waves. I look beyond the water's edge out across the blue Atlantic all the way to the horizon where I see an early morning sky the color of pewter streaked with pale pink. I know not what lies beyond that place where sky meets water to draw a horizontal line as far as I can see. I know not what lies beyond tomorrow or even what the next hour holds. I don't know that vacation activities at this condo will soon be abruptly halted.

The roar of the ocean pulls my attention back to the beach itself. There, I see people have formed into a large group. A man points toward our condo, and everyone in the circle looks in the direction he's indicated. Then I hear the faint sound of the doorbell and go inside to answer it. When I open the door, facing me is a young woman with straight blond hair. She wears a billed cap, white T-shirt, and green shorts. Stumbling over her words, she tells me that a nine-year-old boy has disappeared. He's been gone for two hours. A stranger to the family of the boy, she is nonetheless doing her part to help. Other strangers, as they hear the news, stop their vacation activities. They come out of their apartments to help search the halls of every floor. They walk up and down the beach looking for Sean, a skinny boy last seen wearing a red T-shirt and yellow bathing trunks. I leave and go to the parking lot, even peering into and around parked cars. The police officers arrive and ask questions. It seems the boy left his family on the beach to go to his apartment and then simply vanished. Along with friends and strangers, the officers search the condo and scour the beach again.

At last, Jeff, our son, returns to the apartment to tell me Sean has been found. It seems the boy had walked in the wrong direction on the beach and had become lost. Jeff tells me that when the father saw his son returning, the father wept openly. After long conversations about what could have happened, about the relief everyone has felt, I return to the balcony where a book still lies open and unread on the vinyl table. As I look once more toward the horizon, I am reminded of Stephen Crane's short story "The Open Boat." Its theme is that nature is neither cruel nor kind but simply unconcerned. Again, I watch the ocean's waves, unfazed by humans' recent terror. Mother Nature may be unconcerned, but most people care. In times of disaster, they band together.

Vanishing Point

Two black and white photographs capture my attention. They hang, one over the other, on the wall of my ophthalmologist's waiting room. The upper picture depicts a scene of downtown Charleston, West Virginia. At the corners of Capitol and Quarrier Streets, Cohen Drug Store and Embees, a clothing store for women, are in view. Both stores are gone now. They're no more than a part of the city's past. The scene, then, could be one of virtually any American town in the late 1950s. Most privately owned stores nationwide have given way to franchises and large chain stores. Today, one town looks much like any other. Our town is your town. Almost all the same restaurants, the same motels, hotels, clothing stores, and department chains can be found wherever we travel. Uniformity veneers our country.

In the doctor's waiting room, I stand and walk over to the pictures to look more closely. I see the image of a man who is unaware he is being photographed. Wearing a long black overcoat and matching headgear with earflaps, he walks with his back to the camera. He has hunched his shoulders in an apparent effort to stay warm. His right leg bent, he takes a step and is frozen in time. Snow clings to the bottom of his boot. I wonder where that man is now and if he is also gone like the two stores in the photograph. I wonder if we as a people have changed in the same way our cities have changed. Have we become less creative? Are we now more observers than doers, than creators? I wonder.

Four cars in the picture, all models from the fifties and each one different, distinctive from the other, are on the snow-covered street. Jutting from a building on the left, a clock shaped like a giant cube reads 4:20. In the photograph, time is immobile; nothing changes.

The second print, hanging just below the first, is a scene of Kanawha River. Blaine Island is at the left, and there, part of the Carbide Plant is in view. Over the olive-brown waters, a coal barge moves downriver between the island and the boulevard on the right. In the distance, floating high over the West Virginia hills, angry clouds darken the winter landscape. Here, too, time stands still, but in the real world beyond the images captured almost a half-century earlier, time fast-forwards. Today, changes come about as rapidly as the beating of a hummingbird's wings. Once a major player in the chemical industry, Union Carbide, like the privately owned stores, is gone, just gone.

When I was in college and sitting in a required art appreciation class, the professor talked about paintings, explaining that each painting has a vanishing point. For some reason, the images, framed and hanging on that wall in front of me, reminded me that everything has a vanishing point. I was also reminded of Percy Bysshe Shelley's poem "Ozymandias," which has its own vanishing point. A king, once king of kings, mighty and powerful, Ozymandias has had his image created in sculpture. But years later, as a traveler looks upon the statue, nothing remains but a "colossal wreck," that is, nothing but the legs of the king's statue. All else has vanished in the sands of time.

Christmas in April

Looking through the glass in the upper half of our kitchen door, I watched tender blades of grass glistening in the slope of pale sunlight. It was late March, and there was the same sense of renewal that recurs each spring. Despite the bright splashes of yellow jonquils, though, the winter's icy wind was reluctant to leave. I, therefore, procrastinated once again as I looked to my left where on our back porch I could see the baker's rack with large baskets on each of its four shelves.

Our daughter had stacked three Christmas wreaths on the corner of one basket that sits on the second shelf. After the Christmas holidays, she had removed the wreaths from the three posts supporting our family mailboxes at the end of our country road. I had planned to store the wreaths away for another year but decided to wait for mild weather. One early April morning when the air had finally warmed and new life was stirring just beneath the ground, I still couldn't remove the wreaths. It all happened like this.

I could see from the same kitchen door that new construction was about to begin in our neighborhood. March had ended with such ferocity that I was surprised to see a fine looking couple viewing the site where I supposed they would build their new home. They didn't seem to mind the winds that blew down bare, dark limbs of surrounding trees and moved white vinyl chairs across the deck. Within the next few days, they both came to the site again and again. Then they began to build. Together, the two house wrens carried materials from the yard and took turns placing them in the basket, which was protected in the corner of the porch by the ceiling overhead and, yes, by the three Christmas wreaths.

Then, a few days later, my husband said, "Dolly, I believe you have a third wren out here looking for a place to build a nest. It's on the first shelf looking up at the second shelf, at the same basket, I think."

"Oh, no, Bill," I said, "that's the male wren. He's trying to figure out where the lady of the house keeps the nest."

For more than a month, the couple worked on that nest, and each time, the female would hone in on home base, but the male landed on various shelves looking for home. After several weeks, when both wrens were gone, I looked in to see how many eggs I could find. I saw none and was beginning to think the couple had changed their minds about the basket. I felt at once disappointed and relieved. If they didn't use the nest, I could at last put the wreaths in boxes for storage. That was not to be, however. Much to my delight, I looked in the nest two days before the mid-April snows came and saw five eggs. Now, the expectant mama stays on the eggs, and the mate, who has since found the nest with ease, comes to call. He goes inside the basket and visits a few minutes. Then, he's off again.

Safe under the Christmas wreaths, the mama remains in the nest most of the day. If the wreaths, in plain view, aren't enough to make April seem like Christmas, the snows that have come and gone throughout mid-April are. But that's not all. Our son-in-law is one of the finest a mother-in-law could want, but he has the same unfinished gene that our son, my husband, and most men have. He, therefore, hasn't taken the Christmas lights off the shrubbery in front of their house, which I can see from my office. Since one example does not a case make, I'll share another story. Our friend, Tammy, told us her husband put lights on a small tree in their front yard years ago. The tree, through the years, grew and grew, and its top is now above the roof of their house. The lights, which can never be plugged in, are a permanent part of that treetop.

Back to my daughter's shrubbery: As snow covered the landscape, I called our daughter and asked her to turn on her sparkling Christmas lights. I'd give up and just enjoy Christmas in April.

A Snake's Tale

Before moving to the country several years ago, I was steeped in academia, and therefore gained much of my knowledge from books. Since leaving the city and settling into retirement of a sort, I have gained, on a firsthand basis, a great deal of information from Mother Nature herself. I've learned that some of what I had read about nature as fact was not altogether fact after all. The occasional unreliability of the printed word was reinforced over time.

My first awakening occurred on a sunny afternoon in June. Two phoebes were busy feeding their seven babies. The hungry offspring with their mouths gaping wide were clustered in a nest that the parents had built under the eaves of our back porch. Gathering food, the couple flitted back and forth from yard to nest. Apparently they had attracted another hungry creature because I noticed that the grass near the woods at the edge of our yard parted and closed, then parted and closed again. Like Emily Dickinson, I also felt "zero at the bone." It was a snake, at least a five-footer, and I watched it slither closer and closer to our house. Like shiny patent leather, its back glistened in the spring sunlight, but its movements were smooth and sure. It knew its destination, and so did I. It was coming to my house for lunch.

Everything I had ever read about black snakes assured me of their non aggressive nature. I wasn't unduly alarmed, but I feared for the young birds, the snake's target.

Calling loudly for Bill, my husband, I simultaneously picked up the phone receiver. As I watched through the glass of the kitchen door, I saw Bill use a rake to coax the snake back into the woods. I dialed our neighbor's number. Don, our neighbor, is so terrified of snakes that he carries a long stick wherever he walks in our neighborhood or, better, rides his lawn mower when he comes to our house.

When he answered the phone, I said, "Don, we used to watch *Wild, Wild Kingdom*; now we're in it. If you hurry over, you can watch Bill battle a large serpent."

Before I stepped through the kitchen door onto the back porch where I could courageously watch Bill through my trusty binoculars, Don was already sitting in his truck on our driveway. He remained safe in his pickup. That day, I learned that black snakes can be aggressive if something or someone comes between them and their anticipated meal. With eyes fired with anger, the snake coiled, ready to strike. Only the long-handled rake was between unfriendly snake and fighting husband, who finally managed to convince the animal to slink up a nearby apple tree.

Bill doesn't like to kill black snakes. I've seen him hand carry them far into the woods. He and I both know they are a valuable link in the delicate chain of nature's checks and balances. They feed off rodents, birds, and other small animals. Every living creature lives off other living creatures. Still, I learned that day that no matter what the books tell us about the nonaggressive nature of black snakes, they can be aggressive.

Freddie Flealoader Finds a Home

Freddie Flealoader's name is a misnomer because Freddie doesn't have a flea or tick on him. With one eye brown and the other blue (the bottom part of each eye is white), he looks like a devil dog. His appearance, like his name, belies the real Freddie. Of medium size, our dog sports large sharp teeth that could frighten the most macho of men. Still, he is a gentle, people-loving dog.

Searching for a good home, Freddie came to our house on one hot summer day. We didn't want a dog because we knew the responsibilities that pet owner-ship entailed. As we were trying to figure out what to do with the stray dog, one of our young grandsons fell in the yard and began to cry. The strange dog with the scary eyes went to him, licked his face, and sat next to him, demonstrating deep sympathy. Our grandson stopped crying and put his arm around the stray dog. The dog, in turn, leaned against the five-year-old. Yes, it was a Kodak moment. We knew then that we were about to get a new addition to our family.

We discovered that Freddie had ear mites in both ears and had not been neutered. Also, he was covered

Freddie Flealoader.

with fleas. The vet guessed his age at about one year. At first, we kept him in an enclosed room, similar to a sun porch. He did not like that because dogs want to be around people. We bathed him and treated his ear mites with drops twice a day for thirteen days. We put Frontline Plus between his shoulder blades to rid him of ticks and fleas. After that, he truly became a part of our family, regardless of his size. In other words, Freddie moved into our house. If we're in the living room, he's in the living room. If we sit on the front porch, he sits on the front porch. When we are out of sight, he's unhappy. We have found a true friend in our new addition.

We have discovered that Freddie, just like our former dog that died of old age just before his nineteenth birthday, has consistently given us his unconditional love in return for no more than food, water, and shelter. Had we chained him in the yard to suffer the unbearable heat of summer and the relentless cold of winter, we would never have known the real Freddie. With tender loving care, he has acquired a vocabulary. He understands about a dozen words and communicates in his own way. We understand him. His personality has blossomed. He has learned to jump off the couch when he hears our car pull up in the driveway, and he never gets on the furniture when we're home. He does have a sneaky streak, but nobody's perfect. Besides, he looks so hangdog when caught that we can't scold him.

As I drive past houses with pens in which helpless dogs have been incarcerated, I feel great sympathy for the dogs. They do not get sufficient exercise, and they are not allowed to enjoy the company of their owners and vice versa. I wonder why the owners want to keep dogs outside in cages or on chains. The owners must feed and water the dog if it is to continue existing while, at the same time, they miss the joy of pet ownership.

A Job for Freddie

Before Freddie Flealoader came to live with my husband, Bill; our cat, Elizabeth Tailless; and me, he had been a hobo. You know the difference between a hobo and a bum. Freddie was strictly a hobo in that he would work for a handout. He had no home and, therefore, was forced to go from house to house doing odd jobs in exchange for food and sometimes even for a place to sleep.

After heavy rains had caused some flooding in the valley at the foot of our hill, our good neighbors were cleaning out their creek bed. Freddie came by and began helping them. In his mouth, he carried rocks and debris out of the creek. They told me that he would carry them to the bank where our neighbors had been stacking them. The next morning, one neighbor gave Freddie his breakfast while the next-door neighbor let him sleep on her screened-in porch. For several weeks, Freddie was able to enjoy both bed and breakfast in our neighborhood. Then one day, he followed Copper, one of our daughter's dogs, up the hill and out our road. That was one smart move on Freddie Flealoader's part. He and Copper fought a brief, half-hearted battle as Copper tried to protect his turf. Then, the dogs decided there was nothing to fight about, so they became friends, and Freddie became one of our gang.

Later that evening, as Bill was hauling limbs to the edge of our back yard where he would burn them, he felt one limb almost come to life as it tugged in the opposite direction. He turned around and saw Freddie with the other end of the limb in his mouth. The rest of that evening as they made several trips, Freddie helped Bill drag the limbs across the yard.

It wasn't long, though, before Freddie moved into

our house. He soon learned that he no longer had to work as hard to make a living. The only job he has had for three years now is to protect the property from deer and grasshoppers (he barks ferociously at grasshoppers). Other than serving as guard dog against these two invaders, he does nothing else except eat, sleep, and play ball with one of us. He loves strangers on sight, all of which is going to lead him to his next job, and an important job it is.

Eldercare of West Virginia (located in Ripley) participates in something called "pet therapy." I asked if I could bring Freddie to visit the residents and was told that I could. This means that Freddie will be getting special grooming for the first day on his new job.

He may decide to get other volunteers since we have a total of five dogs among the three houses out our road. Our daughter has a grapevine wreath on her door, and a sign across the middle says, "All Strays Welcome." So far, three strays have seen and read the sign and have taken her up on her offer. Copper was the first, followed by Fuzzy Britches, and more recently by Toby (call name). His full name is Tobias Smellit, a play on the eighteenth century Scottish writer's name, Tobias Smollett. Our son and his wife have the fifth dog, Rocky. Rocky's mother is a Great Dane and the father is a Labrador retriever. Need I say more? The dog is so tall that he can stand on all fours and look the driver of an SUV in the eye. I tried to tell Freddie that his buddies do not have the necessary skills for this very special job. Three are too feisty and one is too LARGE. Only Freddie is qualified for the new job, and he's eager to get started.

The Purple Pill Eaters

"Isn't that awful?" said my ninety-one-year-old mother as she nodded toward the examination table in the doctor's exam room.

It was a question-statement if you'll forgive the oxymoron. She wasn't asking me if "that" was awful. She was stating emphatically that "it" was awful. On the examination table was a protective paper cover, the kind that prevents the former patient's germs from getting on the next patient. The word "Viagra" formed a pattern over the entire paper, which was surely a gift from the pharmaceutical company. You get the picture: Viagra – Viagra – Viagra. The repetition, the advertisement, was supposed to plant a seed of a suggestion in the far corner of the patient's mind. My mom thought that the word and its suggestion were "awful." I thought it was terrible, too, but perhaps for a different reason.

Other drug advertisements were on the wall of the doctor's lab. For example, prominently displayed was the purple pill, the same pill frequently advertised on television commercials. That plastic purple pill must have been four inches long. The male over-voice on a recurring television commercial tells us to ask our doctors about today's purple pill. I don't even know what that pill is for, but I've been told so many times that I should ask my doctor about it that I may have to beg for a prescription or at least a few samples.

We Americans are bombarded daily with contradictory messages. Here's what we hear over and over again: "Just say no to drugs/Ask your doctor about Vioxx or Nexium or you name it."

I know several pharmaceutical sales reps, and they all admit that they have catered to doctors. Some reps are asked to bring donuts to the office or other special foods. Nothing is too good for the physician because he or she is the one who decides which drugs to prescribe (if they're on a preferred list, that is). When I told my doctor that I might write about the contradictory pro-drug/anti-drug commercials, he said that I should also mention the health management organizations (HMOs) and their deals with pharmaceutical companies. It appears that some drug brands are paid for while others are not, so the doctors' choices are limited. At the same time, some drug companies (almost always the small companies) are arbitrarily locked out of the free marketplace.

The cigarette commercials have been outlawed because tobacco is considered to be addictive while, at the same time, commercials have been made legal that promote prescription drugs. I can remember when we never saw drug commercials on television.

Medical costs are soaring. I wonder if anyone is asking why health-care costs are rising at a disproportionate rate to other services and products. The medicine a patient takes should be solely up to the doctor. The patient should not be encouraged by TV commercials to ask about any prescription drug. Do these ads, in any way, help to increase drug prices? Too many of our citizens must do without life-prolonging or even life-saving drugs unless they're able to get them from Canada, where medicines are much less expensive. Pharmaceutical companies claim the costs here are high because of necessary research, but our tax money pays for most of that research.

As my mom said, "Isn't that awful?" It surely is.

Taxing Situations

This is a true story, which Bill, my husband, shared with me. Many years ago, my father-in-law, Howard, purchased a hillside lot on which he built his house. The lot extended down the hill in the back of his house and across a narrow road. During one year, officials in the county where he lived decided to update the appraisals of all real estate. People were hired for the express purpose of re-evaluating property. When the person appraised Howard's land, he treated the lot above the road as one piece of property and the lot below as a separate lot. The strip of land below the road was nothing but a precipice of solid rock. When Howard received his tax bill, though, he discovered to his utter amazement that this unusable piece of land had been appraised at a whopping $10,000, which was a great deal of money in those days. For most of us, it still is. Of course, his taxes were raised accordingly.

Bill accompanied his father to the county courthouse, where the following conversation took place. Howard stood on one side of the employee's window, looking at the confident county employee on the other side.

Howard said, "My tax bill is not correct. The strip of land appraised at $10,000 is nothing but a steep cliff of solid rock. It's good for absolutely nothing. There's no way that it can be worth anything, much less $10,000."

County employee countered with, "Yes, our assessor claims it's worth every penny of that. It is well worth $10,000."

Howard said, "And you're sure that's a fair appraisal? Absolutely sure?" (He was setting up the naïve employee.)

"Absolutely," said the employee.

"Okay, then, tell you what I'll do. I'll give you the

land free and clear. I'll draw up a deed and make this rock cliff a gift to you, and you can pay the taxes," said Howard with a smile.

Shifting from foot to foot, the county employee stammered a bit, but the result was a lowering of Howard's taxes to their original amount before the re-evaluation process, which had been put in motion to get more money for the county.

In the same county today, a debate has been ongoing among school board members who know how to put on a good show. I understand that they yell at one another and pound fists on tables as faces turn crimson with anger. A friend told me that people have even begun to travel from afar just to watch the circus display of human behavior. The recent debate centered on an excess levy. One board member wanted to put a cap on the levy while the others did not. I don't think the board members need worry about a levy at all. They could raise the necessary funding by selling tickets to their meetings. From what I've been told, people would pay exorbitant prices for the tickets just to watch the exhibition. Alas, the vote has been taken, and the levy will have the cap removed. Now, if the people will just pass the levy. Of course, if citizens turn thumbs down, there is always the sale of tickets. I think Howard would have liked that idea. He was, after all, a clever negotiator. Of course, he had justice on his side.

Now there is talk of taxing soft drinks, juices, and powered mixes for making drinks. My husband thinks they should put a tax on beer so that there won't be as many empty cans and bottles littered alongside our road. He's tried of picking them up. These are all taxing situations.

The Case of the Missing Author

The first time I saw him was in the early '70s when he read from a small red-bound book he had written years earlier. His long hair, salt-and-pepper beard, and multicolored love beads revealed his proclivity for a Bohemian appearance. Standing in front of an unusual framed Christmas tree that hung on the wall behind him, he read in a soft voice. The tree full of gems behind him had been glued to red felt and surrounded with a dark wooden frame. The creation provided a suitable backdrop for the reading of *A Tree Full of Stars*.

Of course, I had heard much about Davis Grubb. In 1955, the movie *The Night of the Hunter*, directed by Charles Laughton, was released. At that time, the movie was not a great success, but I saw it and thought it was excellent. Based on Grubb's best-selling novel by the same name, the movie starred Robert Mitchum in what critics now call his finest role. Mitchum plays an itinerant preacher who has the letters l-o-v-e tattooed on the fingers of one hand and h-a-t-e tattooed on the fingers of his other hand. As he preaches, his hands do battle with each other. The traveling preacher arrives at the humble home of a widow with two children. He sweet talks her into marriage, but the marriage soon turns sour. Shelley Winters co-stars as Mitchum's wife, Willa. Not long after the wedding day, Willa is found in the murky waters of a nearby lake. She is seated in a submerged Model T Ford with her golden hair floating upward. The scene is as chilling and memorable as any I've seen. According to current critics, Laughton created a masterpiece. Indeed, Martin Scorsese has restored the classic film. On October 3, 2001, at 9:15 p.m., the International Federation of Film Archives, no less, presented its first FIAF Award to Scorsese for his restoration of the *Night of the Hunter*. The Internet announcement contains no mention of the creator of the original story, the author of the novel. There is no mention of West Virginia's own Davis Grubb.

Shortly after I heard him read from *A Tree Full of Stars*, I invited him to our home for dinner and later to the campus where I taught. In our living room, he talked about going to Hollywood where he came to know Robert Mitchum, Shelley Winters, and other stars. He was consulted throughout the filming of his novel. He shared with us a faded photograph in which he held his small dog, Charlie. His bearded dog, long dead, had looked just like ours, so it was okay when during that evening our dog nipped the author's pants leg. As we talked, I learned that Davis Grubb was well read, but that his life, once filled with glitter and glamour, had dulled considerably.

One dark night, a few months later, as rain came down in torrents, our phone rang. It was Davis. He asked if he could come to our house, reminding me that I told him when he wanted a good home-cooked meal to call me. I suggested that we take him out to dinner. He readily agreed, and a few minutes later he was standing on the appointed street corner in the downpour, where we picked him up. When we entered the restaurant, Davis turned heads, a fact that probably delighted him. With his knitted cap, long hair, and love beads, he walked toward the table with a new manuscript tucked under his right arm. The manuscript would become his final book, a hefty tome, titled *Ancient Lights*.

After becoming ill with lung cancer, he returned to New York to be with his brother. He died there, but his story of love and hate, of good and evil, has been resurrected and praised. Here's to Davis Grubb, the real creator of a masterpiece, *The Night of the Hunter*.

Country Living

I live inside Appalachia. Having resided in a rural part of West Virginia for ten years, I am at last a true countrywoman. This means I know how to greet a truck driver as he passes my car on a narrow road. I acknowledge his slight nod by smiling and also nodding ever so slightly. Or I barely lift four fingers from the steering wheel to return another driver's greeting. I don't always know the person behind the wheel, but that doesn't matter. In the country, we strangers exchange greetings as if we've known one another all our lives.

Before moving to the country, I had read about the Grange in a college history class, but I thought it was a relic from bygone days. I have since discovered that the Grange is still in existence in rural areas across the nation. Our local Grange building is used for senior citizen luncheons, as well as community meetings that focus on topics as diverse as water, sewage, security, education, and political candidates. Oh yes, the building is also used for Grange meetings.

I lead a simple life. If I lived in, say, New York City, I could attend Broadway plays, stroll through Central Park or down Fifth Avenue. I could visit the Empire State Building, the Garment District, or the Statue of Liberty. My life would be exciting. Still, there are things I can do in the country that I couldn't do in a large city.

I can walk off my hill and visit a group of women who hold a weekly quilting bee in a small white church. They serve delicious home-cooked food. I can go to yard sales where I meet and make friends with neighbors I've never seen. Neighbors in the country often live miles apart. I went to a recent yard sale where the man of the house gave me his special recipe for crab dip. His recipe was signed "From the Kitchen of Elmer Bullard," and he was right. His crab dip is the best I ever tasted.

Nightlife in a big city contrasts sharply with nightlife in the country. I remember my first attendance at a country concert. My husband and I had been clearing land all day. As dark approached and the stars appeared, we sat in lawn chairs around the brush fire, drank coffee, and listened to an aria performed by Ms. Whippoorwill. The special music of crickets and other insects accompanied her song. The performer moved from tree to tree so that she encircled us again and again. The whole experience was as delightful as a concert at the Metropolitan; it was just different.

When fall leads into winter and the snow piles high on our road, it isn't long before we hear the engine of our neighbor's riding lawn mower to which he has attached a blade. He drives his mower up and down our road until it is again passable. In the country, neighbor helps neighbor. When there is illness or a death in the family, neighbors and church members fill the house with food. The concern is genuine, and there is always a friend within reach. While I cannot easily attend Broadway plays or partake in other big-city events, I am surrounded by the warmth of friendly neighbors and Mother Nature, who can put on the most magnificent of shows.

In the Classroom of Life

A rotund man with a mocking smile, he was self-confidence personified. Wearing round eyeglasses, the professor had a reputation that instilled some fear in his students even before they entered the room on the first day of class. I sat on the front row of English Drama to 1642. Besides his amused smile, he also sported a large ring on the little finger of his right hand. One week, the ring might be a silver image of Medusa, the next, a jade carving of Satyr.

We read plays by Christopher Marlowe, who was born in the same year as Shakespeare. The professor told us that just as the runner of a race is made faster by keen competition so Shakespeare's writing was made better because of Marlowe, Shakespeare's contemporary playwright. We read plays by Thomas Kyd, who wrote bloody tragedies and was one of the earliest forerunners of the blood-and-guts stories we see on television and in movies today.

I had my peaks and valleys in that class. When I gave an oral report, I said, "Marlowe could tie a Technicolor bow in the tail of the English language." For some reason, the professor liked my metaphor, and I liked the class. That was one of the peaks. The valley came when I submitted a fourteen-page paper on "The Duchess of Malfi." In Charleston, West Virginia, there is a Dutchess bakery, and its spelling had imprinted itself in one of my memory cells. All the way through the paper, I spelled *Duchess* with a t. When the professor looked at the title of my paper, his mocking smile became more mocking, and instantly I knew what I had done. I snatched the paper from his desk and asked if I could submit it that evening. He laughed, but nodded. I must have used two bottles of Liquid Paper to correct all the misspellings of *Duchess*, for that was before computers made writing easier, but not necessarily better. I learned many lessons in that class as I did in them all.

The outstanding characteristic of Dr. H., however, was his philosophy, which stood in stark contrast to most of the other professors. He said one day, almost as an aside, "Ever since the eighteenth century when science supplanted God in the minds of the so-called intellectuals, we've been going downhill as a human race." I've thought about his off-hand comment many times during the following years, which in retrospect tells me what an outstanding professor the man was.

Professors come in all sizes and philosophies. Each is unique of course. Another man taught at the same university and had a reputation of being the "fair-haired teacher who would go places." I stayed in his poetry class for three weeks before I dropped it. Each week, we sat in a circle and guessed in which literary periods selected poems had been written. There was no teaching. That professor was soon hired by an Ivy League university, where he is probably tenured. Dr. H., as far as I know, remained in a university that couldn't compare with the prestige of the Ivy League school, but he was by far the superior teacher. In the classroom of life, then, I've learned that excellence in one's profession is not always rewarded. Dr. H. was rewarded, though, in another way; he obviously loved what he did.

An Orchid, a Man, a Brick House

In the late '40s and '50s, the end-all for most young women was to get married. Movies, magazines, and ads all helped to strengthen the idea that a woman was incomplete until she had landed a husband. But those of us who lived on Brickyard Hill had higher aspirations. Our first goal was to receive an orchid from a date or a prospective date. An orchid back then was a sign of opulence. Eventually, we wanted to land a husband, but right up there with the wish for an orchid was our desire to live in a brick house. The man, tricked into marrying, would be just a means to an end. He would have to provide an orchid first and a brick house later. We dated various shy young men, then, and waited breathlessly for the orchid, followed by the proposal. The brick house, with us, always came after marriage, never before.

I remember the day I was sitting in front of my manual typewriter at United Fuel Gas Company, when a messenger stuck his head around the door and said, "Delivery for Dolly Wood."

I looked up and in the messenger's extended hand was one beautiful, fragile orchid resting in florist grass. I couldn't wait to open the card. It was signed by a young man who, in today's language, had become my stalker. Each time I went for lunch, he was standing on a nearby street corner. He followed my friends and me to our chosen restaurant. He called me each evening, and each evening I refused his invitation for a date. In time, he disappeared from the corner, and I don't know whatever happened to him. That was, though, the last orchid I ever received.

The proposal had not come my way yet, and so I set about, as did my peers, to follow the advice of the day. Now to find a husband, a young damsel had to set a tender trap. The 1955 movie *The Tender Trap* reinforced the idea of tricking a man into marriage. Starring Frank Sinatra and Debbie Reynolds, the film has a plot that revolves around a woman who sets a trap to ensnare a rich bachelor.

To succeed, we women were advised by the experts not to flaunt our brainpower in front of our dates and never, ever, beat a date at any game. In short, each of us was to be no more than a pretty face, and a pretty face was essential, along with gorgeous hair.

This meant putting emphasis on our looks. Each of

us curled our hair in tiny pin curls all over our head. When we combed out the curls, we looked like older versions of Shirley Temple. Later, we teased and sprayed our hair with a lacquer-like substance so that not a single hair would move were we to be caught in a hurricane. We wore spike heels with pointed toes and gladly limped along the road to romance. In later years, most of us would either have foot surgery or wear shoes misshapened by deformed feet. By the time we realized our feet were deformed, the word wardens would not allow us to use the honest word "deformed."

Living now in the golden years with some small amount of wisdom, I don't miss the orchids I never received, and I don't miss the brick house. I have learned that marrying the right man—without trickery—and living in a house we've made into a home by our labor of love couldn't have turned out better.

My Friend Evelyn

Standing tall at 5 feet, 3 inches, she talks true, walks fast, and writes well. Now in her early seventies, she hasn't shrunk an inch. She is an amazing woman with blue, hazel, or green eyes (the color depending on the color of her outfit) and reddish hair, which she often wears in a bouncing ponytail. She's an aficionado of snakes, an honorary member of a motorcycle club, a DWEEB, and sometimes even an impostor.

When my friend Evelyn told me she liked snakes, I said, "The first three letters of your name spell Eve." That didn't faze her. She proceeded to tell me how I could distinguish a male snake from a female (I really wanted to know that). Then she told me about a ball

Robert O'Dell, president of Rolling Thunder, WV Chapter, and Evelyn Smith.

python named April. Doing a favor for a friend, she had baby-sat with April for several weeks. Like a pet dog, the large snake followed her wherever she went. I saw a photograph of April looking in the glass of a door to see where Evelyn had gone after she had left the snake sunning on a rock by her backyard pool. I thought her affinity for snakes was astounding enough, but when I heard she had joined a motorcycle club, I couldn't believe it.

She and her husband, Ted, were traveling and stopped at a motel. To their surprise, the lot was filled with motorcycles and burly fellows with long beards and hair. Evelyn looked at their leather jackets and heads wrapped in bandannas and wondered if she and Ted would get any sleep. As it turned out, the Rolling Thunder Motorcycle Club comprised some of the finest people Evelyn had ever met. When they saw Ted and Evelyn, the members made a special effort to be quiet that night. Evelyn made friends with them during the continental breakfast the next morning. She was so impressed with their patriotism, their belief in God, and their consideration for others that she wrote a letter to the president of the club. As a result, the president invited her to speak on July 4, 2003, in Hurricane, West Virginia. Evelyn is now an honorary member of Rolling Thunder.

She's also a DWEEB. A preacher at her church said he didn't think he could bring himself to call her a DWEEB, but she said, "Oh, that's better than the name we did have. We were called the Four Horsemen." He agreed. The DWEEBS is made up of four women, but one is so bashful that I won't mention the other three names. When I asked what the letters stood for, the members didn't know. My question triggered much thought and finally an answer. DWEEBS stands for Dames Who Enjoy Everything 'Bout Shopping. When Evelyn ordered flowers after my mother's death, the woman at Evergreen Florist in Ripley said, "How do you want the card signed?"

Evelyn, said, "Now, this isn't going to be easy."

When the flowers arrived, the card was signed simply, "The DWEEBS." I'm now an honorary DWEEB.

Then there's the time Evelyn sat at an information desk at the Smithsonian Air and Space Museum and pretended to be the receptionist. She put the "Closed" sign under the desk and proceeded to answer visitors' questions and even accepted and returned a necklace that had been lost. After she rested, she put the "Closed" sign back on the desk and left. That's my friend Evelyn, and I wonder what she's into today.

Age and Years

If you think you're old, you probably are—even if you're only thirty-five. I know folks in their forties who dwell on getting old, and they do appear old. I have other friends in their seventies who ride trail bikes and run in road races and travel and live life to the fullest. Two friends of mine in their seventies, a husband and wife, are even models, good-looking models, too. I don't think of them as old; they don't think of themselves as old. While our bodies do age, we don't have to focus on aging. If we are fortunate enough to be in fairly good health, we can do most of the same activities we did when we were young.

When I hear someone say, "I'm having a senior moment," I want to say, "No, you're having a human moment." People of all ages make mistakes and forget and have car accidents and have days when they just blunder along. Stereotyping the geriatric crowd has resulted in too many members of that crowd living up to the stereotypes.

Here are some tips that will make you feel and appear younger, despite Father Time. What's more, following these tips won't cost you a penny. Keep the retirement publications and all medications out of sight. Walk as quickly as you are physically able to walk. Stand tall. Do not discuss minor ailments with friends. Do not talk about laxatives or irregularity or your appetite or your sleep habits. Never say, "I'm having a senior moment." Never say, "When I awake in the morning, I'm just glad to find out I'm alive for another day." When you get out of a chair, arise as quickly as possible. Learn to part with items that clutter your home and your life. Memorize a poem, learn a new language, or read a book. In other words, keep the mental muscles in good shape by exercising them regularly. Change your routine for a day. Remember that if you remove four of the right letters from the word *routine*, you have the word *rut*. Visit a place you've never seen.

Here's another tip from my friend Barbara. She goes to exercise classes (another tip), and she told me that her exercise leader said, "Smile and look ten years younger." So, smile often. Work on keeping a good sense of humor. Laughter is the best medicine, cliché or not. Make friends with people of all ages. Drown old grudges in the sea of forgetfulness. If you forget something, say it's because you have a creative mind.

If you think you look too young to be taken seriously (I can hardly imagine such a predicament, but I know it exists), then here are a few tips for you. If you're a man, grow a mustache. I know a young man who did this. I'm not sure it helped, but he felt more mature. If you're a young woman, lower the pitch of your voice. Nothing makes a woman seem childish more quickly than a squeaky voice. Don't be afraid to laugh, but halt the giggling. Enjoy youth, for it is short-lived. Don't taint your young years with dread of growing old. Each age has it sweetness.

Sunsets

Sunshine on that fall evening glowed like a stage light so that everything appeared to be coated with transparent gold. By the time the sun turned the western sky scarlet and then slid behind the distant hill beyond our house, the air had taken on the texture of cool satin. It's strange how some events play at the edge of our memories like recurring tunes that echo against our will. Again and again, I think of that evening in the mid-forties.

On that day, I was in my early teens, and I thought appearances were everything. I had received new clothes for my birthday a few weeks earlier and would wear them for the first time. Preparing to go to the United Services Organization building (USO) in North Charleston that evening, I remember opening the large white box that still held my gift. I carefully folded back the fragile tissue paper and retrieved a pink long-sleeved knit shirt with its turtleneck. I found in the bottom of the box socks to match. Aunt Phyllis had also included a plaid hair ribbon in shades of pink and ivory. Saddle oxfords and a black pleated skirt would complete my outfit. After dressing, I smiled at my reflection in the mirror. I was as narcissistic as a teenager could be.

A short time later, four of my friends and I walked down the steep, unpaved road off our hill, up Washington Street, and then across a grassy field to the USO, now the North Charleston Recreation Center. We entered the building through large double doors. It was a place we teenagers visited almost every Saturday night, drank colas, and danced. We were still young enough so that we girls could jitterbug together while tongue-tied boys leaned shyly against the walls as they tried to muster enough courage to ask us to dance. As Fitzgerald said, tender was the night and tender were our years.

The jukebox at the USO boasted curved panels of swirling orange and yellow. It held long-playing records of big band tunes by leaders like Tommy Dorsey and Glenn Miller. Some songs were suited for slow dancing, others for jitterbugging. That night, I remember dancing the entire evening away and walking happily back up the dark hill toward home with my friends.

For many years since then, I've thought of that night and have wondered why. Now, I believe the echoing memory of that seemingly trivial experience is to remind me of the contrast between who I was then and who I am now. That young girl who thought of nothing but how she looked has long since been replaced by someone else. It is a metamorphosis that happens to all of us in time if we're lucky.

I cannot pinpoint a specific date when I looked in the mirror and saw, much to my astonishment, the reflection of an aging woman. In retrospect, my growing older appears to have happened during just one night. That is not true, of course, but it seems that way. I went to bed one golden-washed evening in later life and awoke startled to find myself an older woman, a person others would call a senior citizen.

During that evening many years ago when I was a young girl watching the sun glow like a stage light as it coated the land in liquid gold, I thought of old age as something horrible, when I thought of it at all. I never wanted to grow old. Now in retirement, I again watch the sun turn the western sky crimson and too soon slide behind the hill. As day moves irreversibly into night, I find a certain comfort in where I am right now.

RINGSIDE

Mother Nature's Diabolical Sidekick

As we go about our daily chores—laughing, weeping, screaming, or crouching in a corner, depending on each moment's event—Mother Nature is continuously playing sneaky tricks on us. Gravity, her diabolical sidekick, never takes a holiday. Covertly pulling and tugging downward at the skin, chin, grin, and other body parts, in time, gravity transforms our former firm bodies into little more than sagging blobs. But gravity doesn't stop there. We get shorter with each passing day. Why it's as if our bodies are sinking into themselves.

Now, those folks who build and market better mousetraps are forever on the lookout for needs they can fill and money they can make. The aging process provides them with endless opportunities. What's more, New Year's Day offers the perfect time for hawking their slimming, firming products. Just when we resolve to eat less, exercise more, and strive for perfection in every area (we do get silly at the beginning of each new year), along come those clever television commercials advertising torture equipment that will transform flab into tight abs and solid muscles, wherever those abs are located. In short, everyone will have the body beautiful.

Of course, none of this is new. I remember that in the mid-sixties when I was still young enough to be unconcerned about a drooping body, I knew women in their early forties who were getting the message their bodies were sending. They began investing in the latest craze, a gadget that a wise inventor had created to put all body parts back where they belonged. These sag-exterminators became as popular as today's treadmills. While attending a meeting of an organization, I first heard about the sixties phenomenon. It was called a slant board. It has long since been relegated to America's growing heap of cultural thingamajigs, but it was a hot item then. I didn't actually get to see a slant board, but a member whose judgment I trusted told me she had invested in one. She sang its praises, saying it would eventually make her look young and svelte again. She told me she used the board every night, for the secret of its success was to use it regularly. The board tilted when she reclined on it so that her head was at floor level and everything else slanted upward as she gazed at the ceiling. You get the picture. She swore by her slant board, but I could see no difference in her appearance. I kept tactfully quiet.

At that time, I was a five-foot-two brunette, and a popular song had the words touting my exact height. I loved telling people my height because of the song. Remember that I was still young enough to be unaware of Mother Nature's sidekick. Now, I'm five feet and one-quarter inch tall and sinking fast. What I would like to find is something that would pull me in the same way taffy is pulled so that I would be longer lying down and taller standing up. Alas, I have found no such equipment, but perhaps those who watch market trends will create a stretching machine. In the meantime, I'll resolve to eat, drink, and be merrily shorter. Maybe, just maybe, I'll resolve to be happy with Mother Nature's transformation, to be happy with where and who I am right now. That's my resolution.

Survival Tips for Everyday Living

If you have ever tried to fold a fitted sheet, you know the difference between irritation and frustration. Before the task is completed, though, you know the difference between exasperation and desperation. Here, then, are a few valuable tips to help smooth away the wrinkles in your day. Whether you're a full-time homemaker, a working wife, a bachelor, a helping husband or a significant other, you'll find these tips to be enlightening.

You might want to draw a diagram as I take you step by step through this amazing feat. By the way, these tips traveled a circuitous route from none other than Martha Stewart, who has received a few priceless tips in her lifetime. Here we go. Mentally label the corners of your sheet A, B, C, and D. Now, take Corner A and fit it into Corner B, which will be straight across from Corner A. Next, lift Corner C, which is hanging limply above the floor, and tuck Corner C into Corners A and B. You should have one corner still out there somewhere. That is Corner D. Try to locate Corner D and tuck it into the other three corners. You're almost ready to place your sheet into your linen closet. At this point, I begin to crumple or roll the sheet into a strange looking lump, after which I open my closet door and give the sheet a fling toward a shelf. I shut the door quickly (before the sheet rolls onto the floor), and move on to something else.

Getting children to behave has been a problem since Cain slew Abel, but I've noticed a difference in the discipline techniques of yesteryear and today. We now have something called the time-out chair, and children love it. I've seen them snicker all the way to the aforementioned chair and smile slyly when they get to leave it. They have learned to complain bitterly on the way to the punishment chair, as they try to hide their smiles. Children know that sitting in a chair is not punishment. Then there is the practice of counting as a discipline strategy. The parent begins with saying, "one" (with voice rising slightly at the end of the one). Then the parent says more loudly "two" and by three, the child is supposed to obey the parent's order. Sometimes this actually works, but I declare that I heard a parent saying "two thousand four, two thousand five." Keen observers know that most children are more intelligent than most adults, and because of their insights, children love today's discipline efforts. I'm supposed to include a tip here, but since spanking might destroy an unruly child's self-esteem and get the parent thrown into the slammer, to boot, I hardly know what to advise.

Childproof medicine containers are a lot like squirrel-proof feeders. Neither works. As an adult, you need a crow bar to get into a childproof container. If you can't find a crowbar, you can bang the container on the side of a sturdy table, but your best bet is to find a small, savvy child. You might try looking in a time-out chair.

My last tip deals with plastic wrap that tends to cling to itself. My daughter says if you can't find the end of the roll, just pick and hope, pick and hope.

Studies and Half Studies

Before you read the second paragraph of this essay, I want you to do something that will require a great deal of mental and physical flexibility on your part. One caveat: You do this at your own risk. Sit on the floor facing a wall; then lay this book beside you. Now, lie down with your back flat against the floor and place the back of your legs on the wall so that the entire length of each leg is against the wall. Next, bend your knees outward and place the soles of your feet together. This position (if you are agile enough to get into it), is purported to enhance your sense of humor. This configuration (*configuration* being the latest buzzword) was demonstrated on one of the morning television shows, and it is supposed to work, for it was based on one of those countless, um, studies. Now that you're feeling giddy, pick up this book and continue reading. Everyone needs a sense of humor when learning about the results of the latest study, so here goes.

Smiling smugly, our son said, "Think how awesome we men would be if we listened with all our brains."

He was responding to the news that yet another experiment had just been completed, the results of which indicate that men listen with only half their brains.

Sitting within hearing range, our daughter said with a knowing smirk, "My goodness, who needed to do a study on that?"

In fact, most of the women with whom I talked about this strange study have wondered the same thing. My female friends all said they have long known that most men don't listen at all. At least, they don't listen to the female voice, they quickly added.

I have a theory about all this, but my theory stems from observations rather than a scientific investigation. If most men listen half-brained, so to speak, then too many women talk half-brained, again, so to speak. When you pair a man using only half a brain when listening with a woman using only half a brain when talking, you can have a serious communications breakdown. Let's suppose the listener is using only half a brain to listen and the speaker is using only half a brain to talk if you're still following me, you can see the dilemma. He's hearing nothing. She's saying nothing, but her lips are moving and words are tumbling out, one over the other, for long periods of time. She likes details, lots of them. He deplores details unless. . . . See next paragraph.

I must say if scientists are going to investigate such a phenomenon, they should study both the male and female listening-speaking skills. If researchers conduct another half study (and we all know they will), they might examine how much of the male brain is used when a man converses with another man. My guess is the whole brain kicks in, plus some extra listening skill from a magical place as yet unexplored. Men don't miss a beat or a detail, especially if the conversation is work- or sports-related and, in some cases, money-related. Our son can tell you every score of every ball game that has ever been played. What's more, he knows everything about the players, and who was traded to which team and for how many millions of dollars. Every man I know can do that, but he can't tell you the color of carpeting his wife bought the previous day or the date of his wedding anniversary, although he was surely at the wedding on the same day as his bride. These are more gender differences, discounting the exceptions, of course.

Oh, yes, to arise from the floor—giggly and renewed like Phoenix rising from the ashes—you'll find it helpful to roll over on your stomach. Then use one knee to get into a kneeling position. If this doesn't work, you will still have intensified your sense of humor while remaining floored by yet another study.

Name-Dropping and Other People Games

Vis-à-vis did it for me. Embedded in the midst of all that American English that the good professor was uttering, the phrase *vis-à-vis* sounded like a discordant note. Frankly, I didn't hear another word because he had tossed into the mix (as the radio talk show hosts like to say) French words. Instead of listening to him, I began wondering why he said *vis-à-vis* instead of *compared with* or *in relation to*. He also had a real affinity for Latin, that dead language still used for names of flowers, medicines, masses (I think), but not for the masses, if you follow me. I asked my scholarly colleague why he liked to spew out foreign phrases, and he told me he did it because he was educated. Well, he certainly put me in my place.

Of course, the main reason the English language is so rich is that we don't hesitate to include words from languages all over the world. Unlike the French, we make no attempt to keep English, um, pure. Boy, is that ever an understatement. Still, we try to avoid using foreign words when communicating unless we want to impress someone or unless the word or phrase is widely known.

But, hey, there are times when we all fall victim to playing people games. Name-dropping is one such game, and writers play this game well. When I'm reading a highbrow book, I soon recognize the fact because it is rife with names of great writers, as well as obscure scholarly authors. The book I'm reading now is bespattered with such names. Here's a tiny sampling: Nelly Sachs (a poet), Nathan Keyfitz (of Harvard), Isaac Luria (a rabbi), Robert M. May (of Oxford), Pierre Teilhard de Chardin (a priest and paleontologist), and Gary Clevidence (an anthropologist). It is a nonfiction work, and some nights my brain has no stomach for it. Other nights, I find it both intriguing and enlightening.

Another way to name-drop is to tell about all the places in the world you've visited. Writers do this, too—some to impress, others to inform. One writer (an informer) tells about visiting the birthplace of Christ. She describes vividly her journey down the well-worn stone steps where oil lamps on stone walls seem to absorb, rather than emit, light. She describes the silver star that marks the exact spot. Fringed satin drapes surround the star. The author says that the whole scene speaks of "grand comedy," so tacky is the décor, but God nonetheless "puts up with it."

We can also drop names of the rich and famous. When I was young and foolish, I connived to get close to such persons. Several years ago, I was in a West Virginia restaurant where a political rally for one candidate was in progress. Telling his entourage that I was with the press (actually, I wrote a column for a student newspaper), I soon found myself sitting across the table from none other than Jay Rockefeller, who gave me his undivided attention. I conducted the interview as if I were working for *The New York Times*. A few years later, I entered (uninvited) a luncheon room where small square tables were covered with white cloths. I sat down at one, and eventually I talked briefly with Gloria Steinam. Still, another time, I interviewed Loretta Lynn on the stage of what was then Morris Harvey College. That was part of my job when I worked with the Appalachian Festival. I've hobnobbed with authors, both obscure and well known. I'm not sure why I wanted to meet famous people unless it was to drop names in a column like this. See, I also fall victim to such folly because the more things change, the more they stay the same, or as the French would say, "La plus ça change, plus c'est la même chose."

A Clothes Encounter

Having wondered for a long time about the difference between a fiddle and a violin, I knew just the person to ask. She plays the piano in the same way Tiger Woods plays golf—that is to say she plays well—very. Each Sunday, I watch her as she sits at the piano and looks out at the congregation. Her fingers zoom up and down the keyboard, never missing a beat.

One sunny summer day at a picnic, then, I approached my friend Sue Boggess and said, "Sue, can you tell me the difference between a fiddle and a violin? I think the difference might lie in the clothes the fiddler or violinist wears."

She smiled and said, "I'll find out for you."

I knew she would either have the answer or would know where to find it. A few days later, she confirmed my thoughts. Can you believe it? A fiddle and a violin are one and the same until the player picks up the instrument and begins to perform in front of an audience. If the performer is wearing bibbed overalls and cowboy boots or jeans, a western shirt, and a ten-gallon hat, the violin is instantly transformed into a fiddle. Members of the audience may clap their hands and stomp their feet to the lively rhythm. Whether they're line dancers, square dancers, or cross dancers (honest), they'll love fiddle music. These people know how to have a good time and simultaneously get good exercise. Yee-haw!

However, if the player is wearing formal wear and a serious expression, you can bet he or she is going to play the violin. Sitting with eyes straight ahead and also wearing somber expressions, members of the audience will probably also be dressed in formal attire. Instead of stomping feet or dancing, they barely move. They concentrate and occasionally nod in approval.

Clothes not only make the person, but they also make those that the person encounters behave according to the person's attire. An example will help. One day I had been presenting a writing workshop, which means I was dressed in my business attire. I wore a red power blazer, dark skirt, and sensible dress shoes. I stopped by the grocery store en route home. It never fails. When I'm dressed for business, no clerk wants to see my ID, and it was true on that day. Whether I'm buying hot sauce or a hot tub, I never have to prove who I am if I'm dressed to the nines. Like the fiddle held by a tuxedo-wearing player, I've metamorphosed myself from a denim-wearing caterpillar into a highly respected butterfly. Metamorphosis itself has a magical kind of quality. So do dress clothes.

A few years ago, my daughter and I went to a shopping mall. We left the house hurriedly and both wore jeans, old walking shoes, and faded shirts. After browsing through several stores, we decided to enter an upscale shop where we found a pair of high-heeled shoes covered with glittery sequins from heel to toe. It was about two weeks before Christmas, and the shoes had a price tag of $600. We picked them up, put them down, and fiddled around the store a while longer. One of us noticed that the clerks were eyeing us closely, and we both knew why. It was our attire. We were fiddles, not violins, so we got no respect. If you want to be given the red-carpet treatment in a store, have your ID handy and wear your Sunday best; that's no fiddle-faddle.

A Mecca for Research

If you tend to be a bit overweight, take heart. If you're really overweight—BIG- time overweight—celebrate. No longer will those of us who have been visited by the fat fairy in the still of each night have to worry. (My husband claims the fat fairy visits me nightly, so I know about that mischievous elf.) Instead of enduring tasteless diets of fiber and water and, here and there, a nasty glance tossed our way, we're going to be sought after, even pampered and loved. My guess is we'll be encouraged to eat a diet of potato chips, hot fudge cake, and anything else that's high in calories. In short, we're going to continue to enjoy life, but without the guilt (if we've ever had any guilt). Running in circles, those fitness-crazed folks wearing tortured expressions and Spandex shorts will no longer be envied. No sir. We, the revelers of life, will be the targets of envy everywhere we go.

What's more, since West Virginia leads the nation in its number of obese citizens, our state will become the mecca for scientists on the lookout for fat. Researchers have found a precious prize that is abundant only in us folks who know how to eat. This invaluable finding holds boundless promises in the field of medicine—a field I know as much about as my cat, Elizabeth Tailless. Since, however, we live in an age of the instant expert, I'll not hesitate to offer my opinion.

As I see it, fat people are going to be rich people. Instead of paying to have our blubber liposuctioned out of us, we'll be paid for every ounce of valuable fat we decide to sell. Here's why. While poking around in some fat that was vacuumed from a live body, tissue engineers found some microscopic thingies called stem or primitive cells. One television personality has called them baby cells and said they can grow up to be just about anything we want them to be. Their potential is mind-boggling. These cells can be used potentially to help bones heal, to replace brain cells in people who suffer from dementia and other disorders, and to replace damaged joints. The potential for helping folks with arthritis, leukemia, and other devastating diseases appears to be unlimited. Actual clinical trials won't be conducted for approximately five years. So, as I see it, we can sell each cell for a great deal of money. My guess is that we won't, though, because we jolly fat folks love life and are willing to enhance life for others, probably free of charge. Drat!

Still, for those of us who have been visited by the fat fairy, we can take heart. We shall soon be able to help humanity become healthier and wiser and kinder—and all at the same time if we so desire.

Art for Bart's Sake

"This one speaks to me," she said. "It has balance, rhythm, character—all the qualities I look for in genuine art. Yes, this one definitely speaks to me, Bart."

The tall, svelte woman critiquing the abstract sculpture wore an ankle-length dress made from oatmeal-colored linen on which were printed gray elephants and brown giraffes. Even her attire was a work of art. Her auburn hair, blunt-cut to end at her earlobes, was stylishly straight. I mean that woman had it all over me. She was so sophisticated.

The woman's male companion wore a tweed jacket with the requisite leather elbow patches, dark blue trousers, and tasseled loafers. He sported a large diamond ring that glittered and glistened beneath the gallery's track lights.

As they walked away and toward the next original creation, I looked at the sculpture for a long time, hoping it would speak to me as well. Trying mental telepathy, I thought over and over, *speak to me; speak to me.* Alas, it remained as silent as a kitten walking on cotton. To me (one who owns not one piece of abstract art), the sculpture looked like a curved cucumber that had grown reddish-brown mammary glands. The "cucumber" was about three and a half feet long, and the glands numbered seven in all. Speak to me? I don't think so.

I have a friend who is an artist, and she does beautiful work. Most of her oil paintings are realistic. I hope that's the correct term. Anyway, a church looks like a church and a tree looks like a tree. Her work is so good that one year a duplication of one of her paintings appeared on the front of a large city's telephone directory. She teaches students in her home studio. Now here's a telltale story that is true. All artists, including literary artists, have opportunities at one time or another to enter contests. A competition for the best abstract painting had been announced in my friend's state, and she had an idea. She suggested to her students that they each take turns throwing paint, helter-skelter, onto one canvas. With a coy smile, she told her budding artists she would enter the result in the contest. She did. It won third place. Accompanying the third-place ribbon were comments similar to the ones I had heard years ago in an art gallery. Like a sculpture speaking to an art connoisseur, that painting spoke to the judges. It had the right balance, proportion, and all other characteristics that make a winner. Imagine that, and it had been just thrown together, so to speak

My friend's story reminded me of the time I read

about an elephant that had created a winning work of art after it had splashed and splattered various colors of paint, in random fashion, upon a giant canvas. Talk about trunk art.

Not many years ago, I was the accidental observer of lawn sculptures. I mean they were there, and I happened to be there at the same time. It isn't as if I had traveled a distance just to view lawn sculptures. Most of these abstract art works were made of metal with sharp points. They could withstand both Mother Nature's onslaughts and the onslaughts of disgruntled viewers. They were, in short, indestructible. I mean they were rugged, heavy-duty, permanent objects d'art. I remember seeing a lone automobile tire that had ruptured. Made of metal, only half of the tire protruded out of the ground. But here's the scary part; it was beginning to speak to me.

Germ Warfare

During one spring evening, I was sitting in a restaurant with my husband. Our food was in front of us and just as I reached for a hot roll, an acquaintance approached our booth. Offering his hand for a handshake, he smiled and greeted us warmly. After he and I shook hands, he shook hands with my husband. Then, we had a friendly chat.

Since reading *The Hot Zone*, a book about the E-bola Zaire virus, I've become as finicky about germs as Howard Hughes, the late wealthy movie director. As soon as our acquaintance left the booth, I reached for a small bottle of germ-killing liquid soap that I carry in my purse. I won't leave home without it. This episode started me thinking about our culture and the many ways in which we unwittingly spread germs.

I thought about reception lines with dignitaries who must shake hands with hundreds of people. Think about the hundreds of people who might get germs from the politicians and vice versa. Politicians deserve to win after kissing babies and squeezing citizens' hands. I'm telling you that it's enough to give us cause to stop and ponder.

Shaking hands is only one of many ways we spread tiny invisible bugs. Sometimes a server (no longer a waiter or waitress) brings straws that are enclosed in paper to keep them clean, but when the paper is wet, the straw is wet. I read somewhere that we should never drink from a wet straw that has lain in a puddle of unidentified liquid that has been spilled onto a tray or counter. The same can be said for a cracked cup or mug. Those cracks can harbor all sorts of microscopic monsters.

Look what happens at a birthday party, especially a child's party. Candles are painstakingly placed on the cake, lighted, and then blown out. The child, often with a runny nose (that's part of childhood), tries to blow out all the candles. Unable to do so, the guest of honor gets help from an adult or two. By that time a fine spray of spittle will have been showered on the icing. Folks, that's the icing on the cake.

Another way we make sure everyone gets our colds involves coffee filters, especially a certain brand. There is no way in the world to get those little rascals apart except to blow on them. It's best to do this when no one is in the kitchen. I saw a gadget advertised one time that was guaranteed to separate these pesky filters. I bought it. It didn't work.

Experts have told us that we should wash our hands

several times a day. Some people are fanatic about it, but what's the use of washing hands in a public restroom if we touch the faucets afterwards? Then, we reach for the germ-infested doorknob as we leave the restroom. The moral? We probably have more germs on our hands after washing them than before. I've solved this problem by using a paper towel to turn off the faucets and to open the door as I exit the restroom.

Like Howard Hughes, I didn't think much about germ warfare when I was a teenager. After all, kissing is a part of our culture, too. And when we're young we surely don't want to miss out on that. When we're older, we think on a different level, maybe not a better level, but different. Kissing takes a much lower place in our list of priorities as we mature and think about viruses and the like.

Now, back to that small bottle of germ killer. Experts tell us that with all the germ-destroying soaps we're using we're killing the good bacteria along with the bad, and that's not good. Before they told us that, though, they sold us on germ-killing soap. Take your pick, but do it with a paper towel.

Brilliant Conversationalists

Talking to myself one day while I was home alone, I said "Dolly, you should write about talking to yourself. Although we never admit to talking to ourselves, we all do it." All that, I said aloud to myself.

Even that famous poet T. S. Eliot knew that at one time or another we all converse with ourselves. Alfred chats to himself throughout Eliot's poem "The Love song of J. Alfred Prufrock." When Prufrock says, "Let us go then, you and I/When the evening is spread out against the sky/Like a patient etherised upon a table," we know very well there is no one else in the room. We also suspect that the speaker is either nuts or a genius, although we'd never use the word "nuts" in this context, of course, unless we were home alone. Literary critics call such a speaker "unreliable," but you and I know *nuts* when we see it. As it turns out, though, Prufrock (like most of us when we're engaged in this sheepish activity) makes a brilliant conversationalist. In fact, the last stanza of the poem is so deep, so enigmatic, that scholars and pseudo-scholars have been trying to interpret the final lines for many years. If you want to have a go at it, here they are—with all due credit given to T. S. Eliot: "We have lingered in the chambers of the sea/By sea-girls wreathed with seaweed red and brown/Till human voices wake us, and we drown."

Do you know what those words mean? If you do, send your interpretation to one of those highbrow literary publications. Here's a tip: Make your interpretation dense by using lots of really big words and sentences that curve and curl around themselves as if they're wending their way through Ariadne's maze. I mean if you stretch the language to its farthest banks as a scholar said to me once—if you make it so obscure that the editor will have no idea in the world what you're saying—your chances of getting your interpretation accepted will increase dramatically. Tell me which editor would ever want to admit that he or she doesn't understand a critic's explication. By this time, you've become a critic (if you have preceded the interpretation by talking to yourself, that is).

Leaving the world of abstractions and returning to the merciful world of concreteness (phew!), I have observed several brilliant conversationalists in real life. I mean I have watched those folks who not only put forth good questions to themselves but also get excellent answers. I remember one bright spring morning as I was riding to church with a minister. He was oblivious to the rest of us in the car, for he was adding valuable notes to his sermon. He was not using a pen and paper. Rather, as he steered his automobile down the blacktop road, he pointed his index finger toward an imaginary congregation and nodded his head toward them. I could see his lips barely moving, and I knew he was delivering his sermon. I think the congregation was really getting it, too. I knew that by the time he was behind the pulpit, his sermon would have changed considerably from the original one he had created. Sometimes, the best ideas occur to us while we're talking to ourselves. I know that was true of my father-in-law, the Reverend Howard W. Withrow. Like J. Alfred Prufrock, he was also a brilliant conversationalist.

In a Class of Their Own

Readers are among my favorite people. Buyers of books, those who want to possess their own "good reads," are usually engrossing conversationalists, whether talking to themselves or others. I have found during my autographing sessions that people who frequent bookstores fall into various classifications.

One type comprises browsers who claim they don't read. They're looking for books as gifts. They often carry slips of paper with book titles written on them. They never stop by the author's table where they could purchase an autographed copy. They would have no idea why anyone would want such a book.

Another class of bookstore visitor is the aspiring writer. One young man stopped by my table and asked me how to write a book. I asked him if he liked words. He mumbled something and hurried on down the aisle. Another young man with purple and hot pink hair that had been spiked into sharp points asked me how I got started writing books. When I told him I probably began by reading books, he lost interest. Several folks at every signing stopped by to ask how they can write a book and get it published. Many have romantic notions about being rich and famous authors. Since I don't have a magic formula for success, I can't help them. Most writers write because they must, and most authors become neither rich nor famous.

Then, there is the superior individual. One such person stood near my signing table but never looked my way. Dressed in a business suit, he had a salt-and-pepper beard. Waiting for someone (I think), he sauntered toward me and was at last close enough that I could speak to him. I asked him if he would be interested in my book.

With a smile, he said, "No, I read only the classics."

I tried to assure him that my little book was a classic in the making, but I knew Mr. Bons would never buy a book from a local author. You can spell his fictitious last name backwards and identify more closely his type.

Admittedly, I have a favorite kind of bookstore visitor. This person is a friendly, smiling buyer with an open mind, a reader who is curious about the book an author has written. This type makes up the majority of bookstore shoppers. These folks buy my book, and many buy additional copies for friends. They return to tell me how much they have enjoyed *More than Penny Candy* and buy even more copies. I like these good people.

Another class of bookstore customer is the talker.

One man stood in front of my table and talked about his life and the manuscript he had tucked away in his desk drawer. Typical of this type, he wanted someone who would listen. I provided a captive audience. As he chatted, he picked up my book, flipped through it, and indicated real interest. After perhaps twenty minutes—while potential buyers waited behind him, finally gave up, and left—the talker put the book back on the table and departed. Still another man told me that God talked to him all the time. He said that when he was debating about buying a new car, he said to God, "God, I don't have no money for that car."

He said that God said, "Son, don't you go worrin' about not havin' no money. You go on and get that car."

I think he was a good man, that potential buyer, but I'm fairly certain God didn't use double negatives. The man's direct quotation threw his entire story in the shadow of doubt.

A few days before Christmas—a time when most shoppers had either grown desperate or gone mad—I had a couple of bizarre experiences. A little old man approached my table. He carried a cane with a silver falcon's head on the handle. He handed one of my books to me and said, "I want you to autograph this to my dog, my parrot, and my cat." Each time he spelled a pet's name, he tapped his cane on the floor. Then, with a final tap, he told me to write "Merry Christmas." I did.

A few minutes later, a young man stood in front of me. He had a long ponytail and hair the color of honey. He leaned over the table, grinned, and said, "Do you know why I'm going to buy one of your books?"

I said, "No."

He said, "Because of your eyes."

These last two buyers are in a class of their own, but they're readers. I like them.

In the Eye of the Beholder

Never could I have imagined it. During the 1950s, my mother painstakingly painted a picture of *The Lord's Supper*. Recently reading a "little literary publication," I discovered that some of those paint-by-number pictures, so popular during the early '50s, have been put on display at the National Museum of American History in Washington, D.C. No, I could never have imagined it. Just think; if we could only find Mom's paint-by-number number, we could offer it for display.

Since I have been concerned of late about appearing to be tacky (I sold two of my books in the parlor of a funeral home), I was glad to learn in the same little quarterly and in the same essay another fact. There is a difference between low tacky and high tacky. If one must be tacky (and it seems that I must), it is far better to be high tacky. I've concluded, then, that I am at least high tacky.

Here are a few other objects d'art not yet classified as low art or kitsch, that is, art of poor taste. All these new terms for art have set my synapses sparking like Fourth of July fireworks. What about those pink plastic flamingoes that we still see in yards today? Will they ever be considered arty enough to repose in some well-known art museum? And what about those replicas of Canada geese poised on front lawns throughout our state? Why, they appear as life-like as the flesh-and-blood big birds themselves. Will those someday be in museums as high art? Then, there are those images of Elvis on velvet. Will they be low tacky or high? I recently saw several velvet paintings for sale alongside a two-lane road. They were keeping company with other merchandise, such as sagging lines of gently used clothing, a baby's blue high chair, and two lamps with bases shaped like women doing the hula. At the edge of the eclectic display and nearer the road for better viewing was a life-sized statue of Elvis. Holding a microphone, he was wearing his famous white costume with sequins. And speaking of tacky, what about those Elvis impersonators? Aren't they something?

Traveling throughout our state, I see other potential art objects that might someday be classified as high tacky. Occasionally, I see a wooden cutout of a little boy with a wide-brimmed hat. He's looking down at a wire just below his waist; it forms an arch in front of him. The image evokes the bodily function. The wood-carvers don't stop there, though. A wooden lady with her back to passerby bends over to show her bloomers. Is this elevated humor? Art? And the black-painted silhouette of a man leaning against a building, smoking a pipe, with faithful dog at the master's feet surely will one day be high tacky. Whirligigs, like tiny windmills, adorn yards and gardens. They, too, are potential objects for future museum displays.

At least one adornment from yesteryear has reappeared in gardens of even connoisseurs of art. The gazing ball, offered in a variety of colors, can now be found in gardens and lawns of citizens from every economic class.

The paint-by-number craze, today a part of our past culture, resulted in art that is displayed not only in the National Museum of American History but also on my mom's living room wall and, I'm sure, in other private homes across the land. The scholarly author of the essay has called these paintings kitsch or art in poor taste. You couldn't have told my mom that, for she was as proud of her work as if it had been an original Picasso. I'm still proud of her work, for taste is in the eye of the beholder.

It's Party Time

It was one of those parties I can't seem to resist—the kind where women sit around and make statements they'd never make in front of their husbands and spend money for things they'd never spend money for if they weren't at "one of those parties." Let me put it this way: I walked out of the hostess's house with a tiny brown bag filled with strange little packages, each containing some kind of powdered mixture. Each package of powder was to be the basic ingredient for a recipe. I looked at my teensy brown bag and realized, once outside, that I had spent more than forty dollars. The night air tends to make one conscious again.

Like all the food-party invitations, my invitation told me to "arrive hungry." I did. We were given samples of each recipe at the party, and when I say "samples," I mean samples. The soup, for example, was served in little paper pill cups that are used in hospitals when nurses with no-nonsense expressions carry them on large trays to powerless patients. The tiny plastic spoon accompanying each pill cup had a bowl the size of a scooped-out pea. By the time I had sampled fifteen or more different foods, my taste buds were on overload, but truth to tell, I was no longer hungry. I must admit that the food was delicious, but whether I would be able to duplicate it in my kitchen was questionable.

The main thing is this. While men sit in tree stands waiting for unarmed deer to come into view or sit in the cold on bleachers where they watch another man carry a ball while still other men chase him, we women are sitting in a warm living room in the home of a hostess who hopes to win packages of the powdered stuff if enough of us buy lots of the powdered stuff. We do, for we're under a spell as surely as men up trees or on bleachers are under a spell. All of us—men and women alike—are engaging in America's favorite sport—consumerism.

I've been thinking a great deal about recipes lately, which may be a symptom of retirement. It is unlike me to think of such things. You see, I visited a friend last week, and she served the most delicious cake I've ever tasted. It was one of those red velvet jobs, the kind a student made for me one time because I had put so much red ink on students' papers, but that's another story. His cake was delicious, too. When I asked him which mix he had used, he told me that his cake was made from Scratch. I never thought anymore about that because I was teaching on a full-time basis and baking a cake was the last thing I had time to do. Recently, though, when once again I encountered a cake that my friend assured me was made from Scratch, I decided to buy a box of Scratch myself. I went to a small grocery store, but the clerks had no idea what I was talking about when I asked where the Scratch was kept. I figured I needed to go to a really large grocery store, so I did. The clerks there said they had never heard of Scratch. Can you believe that? I'll bet I need to go to "one of those parties" where Scratch is sold. If you know any consultants who sponsor Scratch parties, will you please let me know? In the meantime, don't tell the men what we women discuss during party time.

Life in the Movies

Have you ever noticed how different life in the movies is from life in the real world? I don't mean those obvious contrasts when actors are able to ascend buildings in a single leap or fly high in the air or see through walls. I mean the more down-to-earth differences so subtle that we seldom notice them. Think about James Bond as a driver, or any other star as a driver for that matter, and you'll understand what I mean.

When James Bond pulls his sleek automobile in front of a building, even in densely populated London, there is always an available parking space right in front of his destination. He skillfully swerves into the space, gets out, walks straight to the door and enters. Has this ever happened to you, even in a small town? Then there is the ending of phone conversations. Have you ever heard any performer say, "Good-bye"? The actor simply hangs up the phone.

And what about those amazing memory capabilities of detectives and other main characters in movies that leave viewers feeling, for lack of a better word, lacking. The boss reads a long list of names, addresses, phone numbers, and other information, and says, "Got that?"

"Got it," says memory expert, who hasn't taken a single note. I tell you it's enough to give me a complex, especially since I can't remember where I put my cup of morning coffee.

Now I can understand why phone numbers in movies all begin with 555. After all, no one wants his or her phone number broadcast all over the country, so 555 is a safe bet since phone numbers do not begin with those digits.

Weather in movies is another story. Most good fiction writers know how to use weather to enhance plot, place, and character. Ernest Hemingway in *A Farewell to Arms* uses rain as a bad omen. In his novel *Anna Karenina*, Leo Tolstoy delineates a storm outside the train windows to symbolize the stormy relationship that will ensue after Anna sees the handsome Russian officer on the train. We won't even mention her throwing herself under a train at the end. But weather symbolism in books pales in comparison to rain in the movies. I mean when it rains on the silver screen, it rains. When two detectives are parked during a stakeout, and the rain begins to pour, the whole scene becomes mesmerizing. The pounding of large drops on the metal car top, the water washing down in sheets on the windshield—all of this has a hypnotizing effect that rain in real life fails to have.

Then there's the music that gets louder just when characters begin to talk or whisper. Music—ah, music—that's what's lacking in my life as I stroll down a country lane, visit cemeteries, shop in stores, teach workshops, cook dinner, eat out, and drive down the highway. I don't have the appropriate music accompanying each activity. Think about *Raiders of the Lost Ark* when the boulder is close behind the heels of Harrison Ford. What would that scene be without the swell of music as the boulder gets closer and closer?

Alas, while music enhances reel life, we in the real world must make do without it because life isn't acting. Or is it?

Lost Soles

One day a few years ago when our daughter was a career woman, she was dressed in her dark blue business suit and matching high-heeled shoes. Sitting in a booth at a local restaurant, she crossed her legs and bobbed one foot rhythmically back and forth with her pump dangling on the end of her toes. When she uncrossed her legs to stand up, her shoe flew across the restaurant in a high arc and landed with a loud plop only a few inches from the salad bar. Talk about shoe fly shoe; that shoe flew. Anyone who missed seeing the shoe fly through the air heard its landing, so no one in the restaurant missed the flying shoe. My daughter arose and limped across the floor toward a shoe whose sole almost landed in the filet of sole. Limping all the way— up and down, up and down—she went to retrieve her high-heeled pump. She picked up her shoe as though this were an everyday occurrence. Diners, unable to stifle their giggles, had to stop eating as they laughed and watched her put her shoe back on. Head held high, she walked nonchalantly back to her booth.

Another day as she stood in a department store, someone spoke to her. As she whirled around to respond, she said she fell off her platform shoes. Suddenly, she was two inches shorter. She said that's when she discovered she couldn't talk and stand at the same time. Those are her words, not mine.

During one morning, as she hurriedly dressed for work, she chose red shoes to match her outfit. As she walked through a grocery store, she noticed that each heel made a different sound as it hit the floor. She said it was more like clickity-clunk, clickity-clunk instead of the usual clickity-click, clickity-click. Clearly, something was amiss. She looked down only to discover she was wearing one red shoe with a thin heel and one with a clunky heel. One was a Rockport; the other was (she said it) a dollar-ninety-nine shoe.

Now, she is no longer a career woman but is instead a full-time homemaker (which she has learned takes at least as much talent and much more patience). As such, she has different responsibilities, especially with respect to taking care of shoes. Each morning before sending her seven-year-old son off to school, she now vacuums the insides of his shoes. When I asked her why she had to vacuum his shoes, she said because each morning grit, sand, and dried clay have mysteriously worked their way into his shoes.

I've had fun with shoes, too. After my foot surgery, I was given a pair of post-op shoes. They were pug-ugly, but the cost was astronomical. Not wanting them to go to waste, I reasoned they would make excellent gardening shoes. They could be hosed off and dried within minutes. But the real story lies in the feet them-selves. The doctor sewed (as in stitched) two pairs of my toes together—a pair on each foot. As our daughter (you knew she would be back) was attending a busi-ness meeting in Baltimore, she kept everyone at the large table entertained by telling them about my operation. Only she wasn't telling the boring step-by-step proce-dure. Oh, no. She told them about my toes being fused together and how my name had changed from Dolly to Flipper because I could out-swim anybody, anywhere with my new, er, fins. As a swimmer, she says I'm now a "shoe-in."

Orientation Obsession

Orientations are as cherished in our society as apple pie and cell phones. In fact, most persons in charge of any kind of classes or workshops are compelled to in-troduce the classes with an orientation. Attendance for every class member is usually mandatory, regardless of each student's age and background. Sometimes, orien-tations are, for lack of a better word, bizarre.

My first experience with orientations occurred several years ago when I first entered college as an older student. I think I was labeled nontraditional. I remember that on orientation day I sat in classroom after classroom listening—more or less listening—to instructors discussing, well, shoot, I've forgotten what.

Oh, I do remember one introductory session in which we watched a movie. Most of the young students didn't miss the opportunity to nap. I wish I had napped, but I was as eager as a puppy chasing a ball. The film had no plot and mercifully lasted for about thirty minutes, but it was long enough for us to see a man slice a live woman's eyeball with a razor blade. Students who were awake shrieked (predictably), and turned away from the screen with their eyes squeezed tightly shut. I still don't know what we were supposed to learn from that, but I do remember the professor's laugh has echoed down through the years.

In another classroom and at the same orientation, an ROTC representative, dressed in his snappy uniform, stood in front of the room, and gave a promotional spiel designed to entice us to join the military science program. Of course he didn't aim his invitation at me, for at my age I was ineligible. So why was I there? It was orientation, and my letter said I had to attend. Later, as I wandered down the hall with other weary members of our group, I saw the man who had registered me for college classes. He asked how I liked orientation.

I said, "It's great. I just joined ROTC."

I doubt that he enjoyed my irony. I wanted to learn, and I had spent an entire day learning nothing, but I did get to see our tax dollars at play.

My next experience with orientation came recently when I registered for computer classes outside my local area. You can see that I'm protecting the privacy of the sponsors of these classes. You guessed it. I had to attend another orientation. This time, though, I had a fact reinforced. I observed first-hand how society had changed since my first ordeal years earlier. The instructor, a young woman, introduced herself and began to talk about our self-esteem. She told us we could do anything in life if we worked hard enough, if we had a real commitment. I looked around the room at the bored faces with eyes as blanked out as Little Orphan Annie's and knew her words would not change lives. She read us a poem about self-esteem and did her best to instill enthusiasm.

She distributed forms for us to complete. Here is a sampling of the questions (paraphrased), and I'm not making this up: 1. What do you want to do with your life?

2. Check the appropriate block, telling why you are here: a) homeless, b) court-ordered. Other questions asked about our learning disabilities and stumbling blocks in life.

Yes, the social environment had certainly changed since last I was forced to attend one of these introductory sessions. I witnessed no "tough love" during the orientation. Rather, we were told that if we missed a class that would be okay. We could come whenever it was convenient for us and, if nothing else, we could stay just an hour in a three-hour class and make it up later. Moreover, if one site wasn't convenient, another might be, and all the locations were announced. I wondered what happened to the mantra about hard work and commitment. I was sensing contradictions, but all I really wanted to do was take computer classes.

Physical Fitness: A National Epidemic

My friend's bronzed skin and ash blond hair both come from a bottle, but her sculpted muscles come from hours of agony, a price she's willing pay. She's into physical fitness, as she says, and she claims to be a physical person, whatever that means. Since she and I are opposites, I must be a mental person. She does know what and where her abs are located. I don't know what or where mine are, but I'm sure they would offer more than an inch to pinch should I ever find them. Her abs are firm, but she says she's never heard of synapses. I know a little about them, even when they misfire. Synapses are of a mental bent. My dictionary even has a picture of synapses, and the picture frankly looks like abstract art. The best I can describe this phenomenon is that in the brain little nerve impulses, when they fire properly, help us to remember where we've placed our cup of morning coffee. When mine misfire, my coffee fossilizes in some distant corner of the house.

My friend's obsession with physical fitness isn't surprising. Twenty-four-hour fitness has reached epidemic proportions in this country. I mean it's become a real nuisance. Under the umbrella term physical fitness lurk all sorts of products essential to sculpted bodies. If we're going to be healthy, we must do healthful things. To be fit, you must eat a healthful diet and, if that's not enough—and it's not—you must also exercise (ugh). To do these, you must invest in books that tell you what to eat and how to stretch those muscles. You will also need vitamins. You must purchase running shoes, a headband to catch the perspiration (remember no pain, no gain?), shorts that hold the body in a vice-like grip, and a tank top to show off the muscles you're going to develop. There are treadmills and weights and pulleys and other machines of torture guaranteed to chisel the body into a thing of beauty. In case you lose your way, you can hire a trainer, buy a video, a book, or an online fitness program. I have a video featuring an older star, and I declare she barely moves a muscle when she demonstrates her routine. It's my kind of exercise tape. The point is, though, it takes a great deal of money to have the body beautiful. And those before and after poses of those who pump iron! Aren't they something?

Then there's the skin. If we're going to have perfect muscular support under it, we must use sunscreen of at least 15 SPF on it. Experts tell us to use lots of it and often. Suntans are out, passé. My dermatologist has a poster on his wall that reads, "The first sign of skin cancer is a tan." Think about John McCain. According to dermatologists, the tanning beds are no safer than the sun itself, but the bottle tans are OK if they contain sunscreen. This means that over my sculpted body, I'll have skin like an albino earthworm. Actually, I already have the albino skin. I just need sculpted muscles for support.

Soul Searching

Tune in for our special discussion on our evening news; the topic will center on whether dogs have souls. The preceding sentence is a paraphrase of a television anchor's pitch for his channel's news segment. I didn't watch the evening news that day, but the idea of dogs having souls ignited my synapses. I mean the idea set my thought processes in whirling motion.

When I asked my husband if he thought dogs had souls, being another family wit, he looked at me half smiling with eyes full of mischief and said, "If they do, do you think bugs have souls? If so, you're in a bit of trouble because you've killed many bugs in your lifetime."

Both of us decided to give the matter some thought. I began by thinking about the definition of the soul itself. Since I think in concrete terms, I don't know how to describe a soul. When describing anyone or anything, I use any or all of the following: specific colors, aromas or stenches, sizes, sounds, and feelings. But a soul? Does it have color? Does it make sounds? Does it emit an aroma like that of a forest floor in the springtime or, perhaps, of a dog that's just come in out of the rain? It seems to me that not one of these characteristics can be used to describe *soul*.

Soul can be described, though, but solely in abstract terms. Most dictionaries and encyclopedias agree that a soul is the very essence of being human; it is a part of us that makes us who we are, that sets us apart from every other person. The soul is connected with mind; it makes us think the way we think and act the way we act. In theology, the soul is divine and, therefore, transcends death. It is the invisible part of each human, and the soul has eternal life. When the body that has housed a soul is no more, the soul lives on. Marianne Moore, the late intellectual poet, said that only the invisible is permanent; all else is temporary. She has a point, but I'm not sure what she would have thought about dogs having souls.

If they do, what about cats and fish and bugs and bears and snakes? A quick search of the Internet will reveal countless poems, stories, and books that folks have written about their long-gone pets, mostly dogs. It seems they can't bear the thoughts of their pets decaying underground, so they believe that their dogs have souls, and their pets, therefore, are waiting for their owners. When I first heard about the discussion of animals and souls, I was reminded of one of those forwarded e-mail messages I found in my virtual mailbox one day.

Here's the story. An atheist was walking through the woods, admiring nature, which he believed had not been created but rather evolved over eons of time. Suddenly, he heard a rustling in the bushes behind him. Turning to look, he saw a huge grizzly charging toward him. Running as fast as he could, the man looked over his shoulder and saw the grizzly closing in on him. Frightened, he looked again and the bear was even closer. His heart was pounding and he tried to run faster. He tripped and fell to the ground. The bear was right over him, reaching for him with its left paw and raising its right paw to strike him.

At that instant the atheist cried out to God, but knowing he had never believed, he was afraid to ask to be saved, so he asked God to save the bear. According to the canned e-mail, the atheist's prayer must have been answered because the bear dropped its right paw, brought both paws together, bowed its head, and spoke: "Lord, for this food which I am about to receive, I am truly thankful."

I'll bet the news director of the television show focusing on dogs and souls received the same e-mail message.

The Metallic Age

Having reached the Metallic Age, I sense a freedom I've never known. Recently, I even donned a T-shirt without the requisite vest or denim blouse to hide my ever-growing paunch—not that the outer vest or blouse ever really fooled anyone, but I had nonetheless labored under that optimistic illusion. Most us mature women—you men, too, for that matter—have lots of *guts*. I mean that in both the literal and figurative sense of the word. Our thickened waists and hips, thinned lips and hair, sagging chins and creased faces all work together to inform the world that we've been around long enough to reach—not the golden age—but the age of metals and metallurgy (the latter meaning transformation). Indeed, we old folks have gone through a strange metamorphosis. Also, traveling through our long journey, we have gained lots of courage (as you know, the slang term for courage is *guts*). Most of us, then, who have been around long enough to remember typewriters and real letters in real mailboxes have both guts and grit.

I know I've reached that age—the Metallic Age—because I have silver in my hair, gold in my hip (injected there by a gleeful nurse with a needle the size of an ice pick), and lead in my derriere. And, of course, there are my nerves of steel, built layer by thin layer over the years until now I can face most obstacles that might turn a less experienced person into a quivering, cowardly earthworm.

What young folks don't realize about us old people is that there are many advantages to looking like a wrinkled 140-pound bag of baking potatoes. My husband says, for example, that almost anything he buys probably has a lifetime guarantee, at least for him. He says there are days when even a basket of tomatoes may offer that lifetime warranty. As for me, I don't feel the slightest desire to have artificial fingernails glued to my ridged, chipped, unsightly nails. I've seen long, pointed artificial nails that have been painted midnight blue and overlaid with yellow stars. Young girls with skinny

brown waists and bellybuttons sporting tiny loop ear-
rings often wear such nails. Now, who is going to see a
walking bag of baking potatoes when earth is populated with tanned young women wearing rings on their
toes? I'm telling you I no longer need worry about appearance. If that isn't freedom, I don't know what is.

There are decision-makers out there somewhere who
spend time trying to find new labels for words that,
through honest usage, have acquired negative conno-
tations. We can just imagine these important VIPs with
their thousand-dollar suits and Mont Blanc pens, sitting around long mahogany tables and wrinkling otherwise smooth brows as they brainstorm to find an ever-
so-sensitive term to replace *old*. Well, let me tell you it's
time for those youngsters to have another meeting. The
euphemistic replacement, *senior citizen*, has itself become
tainted with negativism. Perhaps it would be good to
contact us old folks who never blanch when we hear
"old" to sit in on one of these linguistic get-togethers.
Since we have learned to cope with most of the surprises that Father Time has bestowed upon us, since we
can solve problems as individuals while VIPs form com-
mittees, since we know the barriers in life's road and
how to overcome them, we'd add a great deal of wisdom to such discussions. In the meantime, as I cavort
through the Metallic Age, I'll enjoy my newfound freedom.

Madness Under a Full Moon

Just try it. Wake your mate in the middle of a long,
sleepless night and say, "Stop that snoring."

Chances are your mate will say (in almost these exact words), "How could I have been snoring? I haven't even been asleep."

When the wheezing, gasping, clicking sounds of one who snores shake the very timbers of your home and you say as much, you still will be unable to persuade your mate that his or her snoring is causing the house to tremble. Savvy manufacturers have produced some kind of little strip that is placed across the nose to stop the snoring. But nothing stops it as quickly and effectively as a full moon.

After all, wide-awake persons do not snore. The full moon ensures that both mates lie wide-eyed and wide-awake all night as they listen to sleepless neighborhood dogs bark and howl at the moon. More cats scream on the back-yard fence. More babies are born. More crimes are committed. Mayhem reigns, according to those of us who notice such phenomena.

Shakespeare knew a great deal about a full moon and its effects on all living creatures. He connected the full moon with madness or lunacy. Allusions to the moon and stars are sprinkled throughout Shakespearean plays and sonnets. The moon especially gets full attention because Luna was the mythical goddess of the moon; hence, the word "lunatic" is used to denote someone who is mad, mad, mad.

I remember my Uncle Bill saying years ago that he sometimes did fall into brief, fitful sleeps during full moons, but each time he awoke, my Aunt Phyllis was awake and staring at him. Of course, he added that she was always wide-awake and looking at him on any given night. She was, after all, a Wood and needed little sleep.

I like to begin statements with "studies have shown" because that phrase, like a cook with a wire whip, makes me look as if I know what I'm doing. So, studies have shown that the full moon has no link to human behavior. According to said studies, during the time of a full moon, there are not more people committing murder or more expectant mothers giving birth or more people becoming lunatics.

Try telling that to my daughter who, like my Aunt Phyllis, lies awake during each night of the full moon. She has also reminded me that many farmers consult the almanac before planting anything. They want to know about the phase of the moon. What's more, many folks who work with wood declare that laying a piece of warped lumber under the light of a full moon will straighten the wood.

Of course, there are mystics who write purple prose about the magic of a full moon. Here's an example, paraphrased according to my moon's cycle: *Let the silvery orb of the full moon enter your soul while you drink in its magical wonder. If you're receptive, the moon will till the garden of your soul.* If you're not sure how to "go with the flow," of the moon's cycles, you can send money to various Web sites for information. Gee, now I know why we don't sleep when the moon is full, all snoring and studying aside.

Just Plane Stories

We had to fly in two jets and one puddle-jumper. Traveling from Charleston, West Virginia, to Iowa City, Iowa, Barbara (my lifelong friend) and I were looking forward to attending a world-famous writers' conference, but we had to get there first.

On the morning of our departure, July sun shone brightly through glass walls in the airport. Blue skies should have reassured me, but no matter how much I fly, each time, I wonder if I'm boarding that "ill-fated flight."

Once on the plane, we buckled our seat belts and tried to look as sophisticated as our fellow passengers. Some pulled out laptops while others listened to CDs, and still others simply went to sleep. They paid little or no attention to the flight attendant, but I listened anxiously. She gave us the locations of emergency exits, but I told Barbara, not to worry. If the plane went down, we'd have no trouble exiting. We'd be blown through the air like a man shot out of a cannon. The attendant said our seats could be used as floatation devices. I looked down and saw nothing but solid earth. Then she demonstrated the use of an oxygen mask, but I could tell that she had given her spiel so many times, she could hardly stand it herself.

I had heard so many plane stories that white-knuckling it seemed rational to me. One story involves the Bermuda Triangle. My husband experienced a horrifying trip over that famous space. The plane hit turbulence that caused the flight attendant to lie on the plane floor on her back as she held onto the seats and braced each foot on opposite seats. Trays of food hit the ceiling, and folks needed bags to get rid of food previously eaten.

Our son and daughter-in-law were en route from St. Martins to Puerto Rico when their plane hit the same kind of turbulence, probably over the same famous triangle. As the plane dropped suddenly, one woman pulled out her rosary and began praying. At the end of each flight, the pilot usually says, "We hope you enjoyed your flight." At the end of that flight, there was eerie silence from the cockpit when one passenger said loudly, "If he says, 'We hope you enjoyed your flight,' let's storm the cockpit and kill him."

Another plane story involves an emergency in the cockpit of a DC 9. The co-pilot consulted an instruction manual, then decided he should pull back a certain lever. He pulled the lever, which released insulation material that resembled feathers. All the passengers were suddenly covered with feather-like material, which made them look like, well, flying chickens.

Our son said that a young flight attendant, obviously new at her job because she read from a book, meant to tell the passengers to remain in their seats with seat belts fastened, but instead she said, "Please remain on the plane until the plane comes to a complete stop." As passengers tried to stifle laughter, she blushed.

Another story is about a pilot who landed his plane so hard that he was embarrassed to meet passengers as they disembarked. They were all gracious, though, but he saw the last passenger coming toward him. A little old lady with a cane stopped in front of him and said, "Excuse me, Captain, did you land this plane, or was it shot down?"

Returning from the writers' conference, we boarded the puddle-jumper first. Just as we were about to take off, an employee on the ground beside the plane yelled, "Wait, Joe, we have to shift some luggage." I gripped the arms of the seat; it was going to be a long trip home.

Hannibal Misses Lechters

Our daughter-in-law cooks the way I do. Neither of us cooks often, and when we do, we give a whole new meaning to the word "potluck." Maybe our diners will be lucky; maybe they won't. Now, before you get the wrong idea, occasionally our diners are lucky. My daughter-in-law, Pam, said to me one day that I wasn't a tough act to follow because we cook alike.

Despite my not being "a tough act to follow" in front of the stove, I love kitchen gadgets. I'm drawn to them in the same way a person who can't sing a note is drawn to the new TV show, *American Idol*. Our daughter, Risa, loves to see me buy new gadgets and small appliances because she knows that, given sufficient time, she'll get them. She cooks often and well. When Pam and I are lucky, we get invited to my daughter's house. Sometimes, it goes the other way around, and if all goes well, Risa gets lucky. She gets to eat at one of our tables.

Before Christmas, I was browsing through a section of Wal-Mart and discovered (wow!) parchment paper. I had read about this strange phenomenon in *Southern Living*. I knew owning parchment paper, like owning a wire whip, would make me look as if I knew what I was doing. Besides, if Wal-Mart was going upscale, so would I. I bought a roll, and when I got home, I told Pam about my purchase. She laughed and said she had bought a roll, too. Neither of us has opened the box because we don't know what to do next.

When bread makers first came out, I had to have one. The first batch was a disaster. I discovered that when the recipe called for one-half cup of flour, I couldn't put another puff of flour dust in the cup. I had bread dough wrapped around my ears before that first sticky batch was cleaned out of the machine and thrown in the trash. After that, I made three successful loaves, but the machine now sits in my daughter's cabinet. I found that it wasn't the best thing since sliced bread, so I returned to the best thing—sliced bread.

All good cooks must have a garlic press, so I bought a garlic press at a kitchen-gadget party. I never used it.

My daughter now has two garlic presses, for I couldn't understand why anyone would take garlic apart, skin it, and squish the buds between metal when one could simply shake a shaker. As you can see, I'm basically a mover and shaker. At the same party, I bought tons (take that literally) of stoneware, which I was told I could not wash. When the surface becomes black and slick with old grease, it's just right for baking. My daughter now has all the stoneware.

Next, I had to have a blender. *Smoothies* had become the yuppies' latest buzzword (in addition to *latte* and *relationship*), and I wasn't about to be left behind in the world of yuppie-puppies. I made my first triumphant smoothie, but it wasn't sweet enough for me. I don't want to drink fruit juices without adding a half-pound of sugar. Sitting on the cabinet, my blender is now a dust-collector.

When Lechters (that kitchen-gadget store) closed in our local mall, I was at a loss. My appetite for gadgets is as voracious as Hannibal's appetite for, well, you know. I've learned to cope, though. When I see a recipe with exotic ingredients like sea salt or fresh cilantro, which requires kitchen shears, we dine out.

Earning the DDDD

Universities should offer a DDDD—that is, a doctoral degree in deciphering directions. There could even be several specializations within this advanced field of study. Institutions of higher learning could offer classes in direction deciphering for DVDs, VCRs, CDs, and PCs. With a little imagination, they could come up with a myriad of classes designed to teach students how to operate other technological wonders, most of which are designated by initials.

I checked a Web site, (which, by the way, is still two words with the first word capitalized), and I discovered hundreds of capital-letter groups, each filled with sound and fury but signifying nothing to me. In the first paragraph alone, I discovered CSTA (Computer Systems, Terms, and Acronyms), TU (Technical Update), and TR (Technical Recruiting). Here's my addition: IDIETDUN (I Declare It's Enough to Drive Us Nuts).

The justification for the proposed DDDD becomes clear the minute we buy a DVD, a VCR, a car, or an SUV. An aside: I don't know how much longer SUVs will be available, though, for the ELF (Earth Liberation Front) allegedly (*allegedly* being my own wimp-word) has been burning SUVs on dealers' lots. I believe the FBI is hot on their trail, but I'm not sure they can do anything once ELF members are caught, for there is the ACLU with which to contend, not to mention all the other initialed organizations floating around out there.

The need for a DDDD on campuses was reinforced the other day when my husband and I purchased a car. Along with our car and all its technology, we received a book of instructions. The book contains a whopping 520 pages of directions and warnings and an index, which as yet has not helped me to find a single topic.

The book contains countless warnings—some necessary, some not. I learned that an inflated air bag could kill me if I'm too close to it. That's comforting. There are warnings about my car's safety belts. If they're too low, too high, too loose, twisted, or not fastened properly, they, too, can cause serious injury or even death. There are all sorts of unnecessary directions. I must not drive with the sound system too loud or my hearing could be damaged. I am warned not to watch the rear video system while driving. I think to do so (if we had a back-seat video), I would have to be the world's most accomplished contortionist. Is it news that steam could burn me and carbon monoxide could kill me? If I strike a match and ignite gasoline, I'm warned that I could get burned. I find page after page of this kind of information. You can see why this tome would make an excellent college textbook.

To ensure that the terminal degree (the DDDD) and one of its accompanying textbooks would meet high standards, there are in the book a sufficient number of initialisms to keep the brightest minds befuddled. Here is a minuscule sampling: NHTSA, TDD, VIN, and TTY. These are all identified somewhere in the book, but it's up to the diligent student to find them.

Oh, one more item: A brilliant engineer sent to me a CD for my computer. It contains pictures, and he said that I might have to adjust the numbers of pixels. He lost me right there, so when I enroll in a DDDD class, I can achieve photos that are pixel perfect.

Chow-Chow or Cha-Cha

When Jenny Carnell was learning how to make chow-chow, I was learning how to cha-cha. Through the years, Jenny has continued to make chow-chow and has the making of it perfected into an art form. Many people enjoy her special recipe. I have never done the cha-cha since taking lessons many years ago while working at the United Fuel Gas Company. The company sponsored the lessons, so I decided to move up to a professional dancing teacher. The last dancing instructor I had was Cat Eye's daughter, and I learned to jitterbug in Cat Eye's beer joint (before it was open for business) when I was a child. Since taking company-sponsored ballroom dancing lessons years ago, not one person has asked me to cha-cha. I have concluded, then, that chow-chow is more important than cha-cha. My Grandmother Frame made chow-chow, but I hadn't thought about the delightful relish since childhood.

At a church dinner where my husband and I had filled our plates with some of the best cooking this side of the Mississippi, Bill said, "I'd give a hundred dollars for a jar of that chow-chow."

After tasting it, I agreed. The dictionary describes chow-chow as diced vegetables that are pickled in mustard. I know that Jenny's recipe has just the right amount of pickling juice, which gives her relish a special flavor. If, however, there is any mustard in her chow-chow, I couldn't detect it.

After sampling most of the foods at the church dinner, we sat around long tables and talked. The conversation soon wilted what self-esteem I had left (you know about self-esteem, a most important character trait). Mary Casdorph sat next to me, and I soon discovered that while she was learning how to bake various kinds of breads, I was buying a bread machine. I asked if she used a bread machine, and I declare that I heard a barely audible gasp from every seasoned cook around that table. Eyebrows arched, and there was an awkward moment of silence.

You're not going to believe this story, but it's true.

Mary said, "No, I never use a bread machine (there were smiles and nods of approval). I have been taking lessons from a chemist who became interested in the various chemical reactions when mixing ingredients for different kinds of home-baked breads."

"Really?" said I.

"Oh, yes, it's most fascinating," said Mary.

Recently, I was talking by phone to a friend who has enjoyed country living far longer than I. She said, "We've been pulling honey all afternoon, and I'm exhausted." This time, I didn't bite. I didn't ask what she meant by pulling honey, although I had no idea. Sometimes, I pull a jar of honey off the shelf in a grocery store. Maybe that's what she meant, but somehow I doubt it.

Oh, about that wished-for jar of chow-chow for which my husband would gladly have paid a hundred dollars. Jenny brought a jar to Sunday school, especially for us. She said, "It is a gift of love."

Life can be sweet.

Back to the Dark Ages

A few friends who claimed to have been spiritually intimate with the late Princess Diana, planned a séance. I don't know what was involved in the planning stages, but I can imagine. Probably the room had to be darkened with only black candles glowing dimly. The séance leader had to create the proper ambiance. Otherwise, Princess Di would refuse to make an appearance, which would embarrass the channeler.

Poor Princess Di has much in common with Elvis, the king of rock, in that she continues to reappear. Folks just won't let her rest in peace. I compare all this with Elvis because one morning as I was driving to work, I was behind a dusty van. In the dust on the two back doors were the crudely written words, "Elvis is in here. Follow me." I was sorely tempted but had classes to teach, so the van went one way and I went the other.

When I mentioned the experience to my students, I discovered that some of them had already seen Elvis in various places, but mostly in fast-food restaurants. I'm going to continue to be on the lookout.

Now hearing about the effort to contact Princess Di on the other side reminded me of my childhood, which was back in the dark ages, more or less. When I was about eleven, my mom knew a woman, one Mrs. D., who had rapping spirits in her house. Sometimes, Mrs. D. even held séances and supposedly communicated with the dead. She lived in a small frame house, which gave no indication from the outside that it was home to all sorts of dark, mystical happenings and out-of-this-world spirits. Grieving survivors from near and far visited that little house, paid some money, and communicated with their lost loved ones. Can you imagine how, with wide-eyed wonder, I listened to such stories? My mom and I visited Mrs. D. one day, and all I remember is that they shared a pot of coffee and some juicy gossip.

Back to the Princess: Oonagh, in her planning stages, decided that hosting a pay-for-view séance on television would be best. As my friend from Britain might say, "Folla the dollah, honey." Oonagh claims that the Princess contacted her (from the other side, of course), so that Oonagh could tell the world about the real Diana. I don't know what happened during the séance because I wasn't about to send my fourteen plus dollahs in that direction. The séance participants held some, um, lofty titles for such an event. Here's the lineup: Princess Di's personal astrologer, a clairvoyant channeler, and a psychic.

In a large bookstore recently, I watched a couple (one was probably the significant other to the significant other) as they browsed. They first scanned the New Age books, then quickly moved on to the occult. The woman wore a long crumpled skirt of purple cotton, a tie-dyed T-shirt of psychedelic colors, and brown manly looking sandals from which large toes pointed toward the man with her. She pulled a book from the shelf and opened it. The title was something like this: "How to Turn a Nice Witch into a Wicked Witch." She placed the open book under her significant other's face. They stood there reading a few minutes, then smiled and nodded to each other.

From the Age of Enlightenment, we had taken a tiny step forward, but now it seems we've taken a giant leap backwards—all the way to the Dark Ages. Realizing this, I left the bookstore in search of Elvis.

Mush or Grits

The dictionary gives virtually the same definitions for the words *mush* and *grits*. Both dishes are defined as white corn meal that has been ground and boiled in milk or water, then eaten. Through the years, I have wondered if the two were the same. My grandfather loved mush, but had we lived in the Deep South, he would have loved grits. Loving either or both helps to mark the Southerner. Preferring one to the other, though, helps to distinguish the Upper Southerner from the Deep South Southerner.

Moving from West Virginia to New Orleans helped me to understand more fully the contrasts between the two states, as well as their similarities. One of the most noticeable differences is in the terrain of each. West Virginia's terrain, like crumpled paper, peaks into hills and mountains, then dips into hollows and valleys.

When torrential rains fall and muddy water gushes down mountain streams, floods threaten the valleys. The topography in and around New Orleans—as smooth as the surface of an unruffled lake—lies as flat as a kitchen floor. Situated below sea level, "the city that care forgot" is also susceptible to flooding when hurricanes pound the area.

We lived for almost four years in LaPlace, Louisiana. A small community, it is located adjacent to Airline Highway and only a few miles north of New Orleans. At the outset, our neighbors welcomed us into the community. They were friendly, hospitable, and generous. In short, they were Southerners, although many were converted Northerners who had taken on the South's easy-going manners and lifestyle.

Instead of the typical West Virginia pinto beans with fried potatoes and cornbread, the main staple in Louisiana is red beans and rice. A delightful Italian lady who lived next door shared her recipe with me. Also, I soon discovered that shrimp didn't have to come in frozen packages. Of course, West Virginia has restaurants that serve fresh seafood, but it must be flown in. In New Orleans, residents actually wait for the shrimp boats, and the shrimp was like nothing I had ever tasted. It was in LaPlace that I learned about mirlitons (vegetable pears). I also discovered that a mixture of browned bacon grease, flour, salt and pepper in a skillet is known as a roux (pronounced *roo*). I learned how to prepare both Cajun and Creole dishes, but the most unusual food to which I was introduced was crawfish. One sun-drenched afternoon, another neighbor gave us dozens of boiled crawfish. She had wrapped them in newspaper and sent the special gift to us by her seven-year-old son. Beneath a blue summer sky, he taught us how to crack them open. Although crawfish are now served in fine restaurants, they were first eaten out of desperation during the Great Depression.

Then, there were the snakes. Oh boy, but were there ever snakes. We lived within a five-minute drive from a snake farm. Deep, round pits made of concrete held thousands of brown water moccasins. A large glass cage held King Cobra, and another cage made of heavy steel bars held a gorilla. The gorilla smoked cigarettes and snuffed them out in his private water fountain. Afterwards, he drank water, raised his head, smiled at onlookers, and sprayed a mouthful of water all over them. Then, patting his chest and giggling like a hyena, he jumped up and down in obvious glee. Whereas Louisiana has several poisonous snakes, West Virginia has only two, and it doesn't have that practical joker, the gorilla.

The entire South is populated with warm, friendly people, most of whom like either mush or grits. Oh, yes, a favorite recipe made of mush has long been popular in the Deep South. The johnnycake or hoecake is also known as mush bread, but the Southerner, regardless of location or food preference, is still a Southerner.

Green and White and Read All Over

What's green and white and read all over? Give up? It's those green and white signs you see along West Virginia's interstates. I don't mean the ones that tell you how many miles you must travel to arrive at your destination or the ones that name destinations. Oh, no, I mean those strange signs that imply we're undergoing swift economic progress.

One such sign, which has been duplicated and placed in countless locations, declares each area to be a

"Certified Business Location." Impressive, yes, but what does it mean? When I inquired about this sign, I was told that the county officially designated as "certified" is the county that will receive preference in getting money to lure businesses (jobs) into the area. But there's a hitch. The ultimate goal is to make each of our fifty-five counties certified for business. How, then, does one county receive preference over another if all are certified? Anyway, where's the beef? I've seen few results.

Another sign reads, "Entering Polymer Alliance Zone." Entering what? The twilight zone? Until recently, I had no idea what this sign meant, and most citizens, if asked its meaning, would probably also plead ignorance. Two articulate persons, though, have within the past few days tried to explain Polymer Alliance to me. One person said, "It's a complicated concept." The one comment, though, that sticks in my mind, like a thorn in a sore finger, is that this Polymer Alliance endeavor is state-funded. As I understand this complex project, an alliance exists among companies in Wood, Mason, and Jackson Counties that, when they combine their efforts, will result in a plastic recycling plant. That plant, I further understand, is still two years down the road. The signs and idea have been in place for many years.

Economic development, like faculty development, is full of sound and fury but signifies little. When I was a faculty member in higher education, we were repeatedly subjected to "faculty development" workshops. I was skating as fast as I could already, but what the phrase really meant was that we professors were to do more for less. Nothing changed, however, which is my point. The ineffective professors remained ineffective, and the hard workers continued to do what they had always done, work hard. But the decision-makers felt better about themselves after said workshops. The phrase *economic development* makes West Virginia's officials feel better, too. Still, we remain at the bottom of almost every list with respect to per capita income, job opportunities, and the like.

Older West Virginians can remember when they waited for the hard road to come through. Then, they thought prosperity would follow. We now have interstates that connect us to the rest of the country. Moreover, we're wired to the rest of the world, but we're still waiting for prosperity.

Admittedly, our leaders have brought in new jobs. The Toyota factory is probably the single shining example. Most of the jobs, however, provide a larger tax base as opposed to providing decent-paying jobs for our people. Here are examples of typical jobs state government has brought to West Virginia: telemarketing and retailing (retail jobs will expand if Victoria's secret mall in Wheeling comes to fruition), betting and burger-flipping, gray machines and green signs, lotteries and losers.

Almost every time a building in the Charleston area is vacated by private business, state employees quickly fill it because our state government continues to spread like destructive mildew. We could have one of the richest states in the nation because of our timber, gas, and coal, but, alas, out-of-state companies own most of our natural resources. We need more than green and white signs that are read over and over again—much more.

Gullible's Travels

This is only a guess, but I don't think a single fifth grader noticed the color of the sky or the scenery beyond the large bus windows. My daughter had invited me along, saying that it would be fun. You can see how gullible I am, so I arose at five in the morning—before first light—and boarded the bus at seven. En route to the zoo in Columbus, Ohio, our bus held (in addition to a busload of lively students) one dedicated teacher, several parents, and at least a couple of courageous grandparents.

It had been many years since I had ridden a chartered bus, and I noticed stark differences between what was then and what is now. The young charges, for which teachers and parents were sharing a long day, entertained themselves with the help of technology. I mean they held in their palms tiny electronic gadgets on which they punched even tinier buttons. Their heads bent forward, brows wrinkled, and eyes focused on miniature screens, they played games. When they tired of those, they moved to portable CD players. They had plastic cases that unzipped to reveal as many as five or six CDs. With headphones in place, various young travelers closed their eyes and nodded their heads to the beat of the music. Sometimes, they even traded CDs. When they grew weary of the music, they could watch one of two television sets attached to the bus's ceiling. Movies, cartoons, and documentaries played on the TV screens almost constantly from the time we left the schoolyard until we returned. I found myself watching Disney movies with an interest I never thought I'd have.

It was at the zoo itself, though, where my endurance was put to the test. I now know that if my car ever breaks down in Charleston, West Virginia, I can walk the twenty-five miles home to Goldtown, USA, without a hitch (no pun intended). We began walking at ten o'clock and walked nonstop (more or less) until four in the afternoon. We walked across rustic boarded walks that spanned bodies of water. Beneath the walks, large alligators gazed up at us with dull, bulging eyes. We walked through cool buildings where various forms of wildlife turned their backs on us. We saw bison and bears, gazelles and geckos, snails and snakes. I learned that one type of cobra is lavender at birth but turns gold as it matures. Trust me; it was mature as it slithered in its climate-controlled cage behind heavy glass.

We saw a gorilla that was a dead ringer for King Kong. With large brown eyes and a countenance that only a mother could love, "King Kong" stared into my eyes, gazed at my wrinkled face, and I declare, fell in love with me for my beauty. He rummaged around eating some type of lettuce, but as soon as he found another lettuce leaf, he'd raise his head and stare into my eyes. I left the gorilla building early on. With luck, I would have three seconds and two ticks to rest on a bench before the gang could catch up with me. After all, my breakfast on the bus had consisted of only a cold Pop-tart and a few ridged potato chips. I was running, I mean walking, on empty.

As evening approached, I realized that in this world filled with trials and troubles, there are still good people—some young, some in between, and some old. I know because I had just spent a day with them and had fun doing so. Before entering middle school, the young graduates were enjoying their last outing sponsored by Kenna Elementary School in Jackson County. As we boarded the bus to return home, I knew it didn't matter whether they nodded heads in beat to music or even saw the sky. They had their heads on straight and their feet on solid ground.

Bring It to the Table

Each year, Valentine's Day comes along just in time to save us from ourselves. It mercifully releases us from our diets begun right after the first of the year. Moreover, we reason that if we stop dieting, we might as well stop exercising (if we've gone to that extreme). Eating chocolates from a large heart-shaped box has a way of halting any kind of fasting. No more lettuce, celery, garbage soup, and those ever-present bottles of water for us. It's high time to get back to comfort food. Yes!

Valentine's Day or not, we humans love to eat far too much to stay on diets for any length of time. Why we like to eat so much that, unlike rabbits, we'll eat just about anything, including both flora and fauna. People from around the world devour meat from all sorts of creatures: horses, cows, hogs, deer, dogs, chickens, turkeys, turtles, and snakes. Even ants and grasshoppers are not safe from the human appetite. Whether fish or fowl, reptile or rabbit, they all provide food for our tables.

Why in West Virginia, our legislators, during one strange session, even passed a law making it legal (I'm not kidding) for us to scrape road kill off the pavement, take it home, cook and eat it. I don't know anyone who has actually done this, but to do so is nonetheless now legal.

To mask what we eat, we've come up with some clever words. Calamari, served in the finest restaurants, is squid. Beef is cow, pork is pig, and venison is deer. I'm not sure what folks in other parts of the world call horses, cats, and dogs when they're killed, cooked, and eaten. I do know that food has become an obsession. Even diets are all about food, about counting calories and points and fat grams.

When we're not eating, we're talking about eating. Allusions to dining have fattened our lexicon in the same way food has fattened our bodies. Think about it. When folks are too busy to help with a project, they might say, "I already have a full plate." When they want to mull over a problem, they say, "I'll chew on it." When they have merely chitchatted or gossiped, they say, "We just chewed the fat." When planning for a meeting to discuss a particular topic, the planner says, "Let's bring it to the table." Poets have compared women to food. In poetry, women have lips like cherries and a complexion like peaches and cream.

I remember when the program known as Neighborhood Watch was in full swing. We saw signboards, each with a cartoon-like dog featured. The caption asked us to "take a bite out of crime." Sometimes, we "bite off more than we can chew," so some projects must be kept "on the back burner." And when a problem fills our minds, we say, "It's gnawing at us."

My grandmother used to say, after hearing a bit of, well, "juicy" gossip, "Now, that's ham fat for the fire."

Of course, Valentine's Day doesn't save everyone, for some folks need to be saved from fasting. Our daughter never, ever, needs to diet so she could enjoy chocolates without guilt. Thinking of the agony men endure on these holidays, though, she said to her husband, "Don, I'm not getting you anything for Valentine's Day, so you don't have to get anything for me. How's that?"

Tapping her lightly on the upper arm with a loose fist, he tossed her a relieved smile and said, "Risa, you're all right."

Computer Blues

Before the computer classes my husband and I took from an instructor with a terrific sense of humor (my former colleague, my husband, and I were in the class, so she needed it), I had never heard of the word *defragment*. When she first told us we needed to defragment on a routine basis, I thought she was talking about defragging our nerves—or maybe hers. As weeks passed, though, the light bulb finally flashed, and I realized it was our computers that needed to be periodically defragged (a shortened version of the word). I was told one time to use a new word often, so bear with me because d*efrag* is a neologism for me. *Defrag* means that if I push the right keys, tiny blocks will form all over my computer screen and continuously readjust themselves into different patterns. This process takes at least a half-hour or more, depending on how much defragging is needed. Here's a tip from a computer-class graduate, who if graded, would have received a D-, so take the tip at your own risk. I think defragging means to get all the documents and programs in the right order so you won't have wasted blank spaces in your computer. Your computer is supposed to work more efficiently after it's been mercifully defragged.

Although I had been using computers for years, I took the beginning class; otherwise, I would have missed defragging altogether. Now a computer graduate with a certificate and everything, I'm still baffled about fatal errors. I know what happens if a doctor or a cook or a lawyer or anyone else not in front of a computer makes a fatal error. I mean I do know what *fatal* means. Sometimes my computer shoots a message to me that's been sent by someone whose name is close to

Demon. Demon exists somewhere in the hot depths of my computer, and I can never respond to him, for he doesn't accept messages. Believe me, there's no two-way conversation with Demon. Whatever fatal error I've made, then, remains intact. No corrections are allowed, so my error is forever deadly.

If I'm not making mortal mistakes, I'm committing illegal acts. I'm not kidding. Actually, the computer takes the blame for the illegal acts, but it will not accept responsibility for any fatal faux pas. By the by, my computer puts a green squiggly line under *will* in the preceding sentence, which meant I'd made another mistake, only not fatal this time. When I checked to see what my computer wanted me to do with *will*, it suggested I make it plural. (If I had followed the computer's orders, the sentence would read "it wills not accept. . . .") The moral to this story is never, ever, pay attention to your grammar software. It knows naught, zilch, nothing, nada. Honest. I hope you're convinced of this.

After learning about your fatal flaws and illegal acts and after looking at so many red and green squiggly lines under words you've misspelled or misused (according to your computer), you'll want to stop writing altogether, which brings us to the mouse and the mouse pointer. You move the mouse on a little felt pad until the pointer is on the *start* icon. In other words, to stop, you click *start*. If this makes sense to you, you're ready for the intermediate computer class.

Like a Bolt out of the Pew

It was three days before Christmas, a Sunday morning. My husband and I approached the church (where everyone can sing except our family members, but that's another story). On the end of the church porch away from the door where friendly greeters awaited our arrival, stood Jo Chenoweth, a friend and church member. She was smiling like a Chessie cat. At her feet was a young character dressed in a yellow and white fur coat with yellow eyes that matched exactly the yellow of the coat. Jo's companion seemed to appear on that porch like a bolt out of the pew.

Jo gave me a come-here-a-minute grin, and I made an innocent walk toward her. She introduced her little friend. I saw that her sidekick could not speak a word of English. As the kids would say, though, not to worry. Jo was an excellent interpreter. She said, "Dolly, this little cat is homeless, and I'm pretty sure it's a girl."

The most big-hearted person I know, Bill, my husband, was standing nearby. Without the slightest hesitation, he looked down at the cat, who was giving a silent meow, and said, "Dolly, let's take her home."

The deal was sealed within a few minutes. As we departed the church, we again approached Jo, who was now armed with a towel-lined box and, well, "her." I don't remember who carried the box full of cat to our car. I remember only sitting in the back seat with the box beside me. It was a shallow, lidless box, so as soon as Bill started the car engine, she climbed out of her box and onto my lap. She purred loudly all the way home. I knew then that we had an unusual cat, for most cats scream and butt their heads into the glass windows in an attempt to escape.

I decided to name our new addition Mary Christmas. When we arrived home, Freddie Flealoader, our curious mid-sized dog, greeted Mary. After Mary slapped him in the face three times, he backed off, but I noticed that his tail was still wagging enthusiastically.

Joseph Leon.

It was not long before Mary was pulling Fred's head toward the floor. Lying on her back, Mary proceeded to wash Fred's ears. He stood quietly, with head bowed, smiling broadly. From that moment on, they were the best of friends. They romp and play, chasing each other throughout the house.

On that fateful Sunday, we still had another surprise. Observing closely, we discovered that "she" was not a "she." We had a young fellow on our hands, which meant the name had to be changed. We tried several names on our tomcat, including Nicky (St. Nicholas). Nothing seemed to fit. Then, the light bulb flashed, and we named our adopted boy Joseph Leon. I reasoned that the first two letters of the name would be in honor of Jo with her Chessie-cat grin and, of course, for THE Joseph. Leon is Noel spelled backwards, so Leon is "his" call name. Since he was a Christmas gift, a name associated with Christmas seemed appropriate.

We guessed Leon's age at about a year. At any rate, we knew he was old enough for corrective surgery—that is, the vet would remove any, um, appendages that might result in other homeless, frightened, starving kittens. Of course, that would be difficult, for Leon is an indoor cat. Still, being savvy about animals, we had him neutered. After the surgery, the woman at the vet's office carried Leon toward us. She smiled and said, "The doctor says that Leon is an unusual cat, a good cat." We knew that.

Love Is a Many-Splintered Thing

A friend and fellow writer says that the word "love" is the most abused word in the English language. He has a point because too many people casually say—sometimes even to virtual strangers—"I love you." All of this set me to thinking about the nature of human love and how it comes in many forms.

There's the five-star mother who loves her children unconditionally. She expects little or nothing in return for a love that flows from her as naturally as the rains fall from heaven. An outstanding father loves his children in the same way. Sometimes the meanest and least appreciative child receives most of the parents' love. It is, then, good that a parent's love is the purest form of mortal love.

Love for a spouse is a different type altogether. Much is expected in return for such love. Any husband or wife insists that his or her love be returned. Many qualities are required of a spouse: fidelity and honesty and support and patience and understanding. The list is endless. Love in marriage then is reciprocal. If you love me, I'll love you. It is a complicated love.

My husband and I celebrated our forty-eighth wedding anniversary on July 18. When we took our wedding vows forty-eight years earlier in my Aunt Phyllis's two-story white house, we meant for our marriage to endure until only death would separate us. In those forty-eight years, I've learned something about the nature of marriage and the love that accompanies it. I've learned that honeymoons do not last, which is fitting. The first year of our marriage, I expected to be told almost daily that I was loved. I wanted to be reassured. Mercifully, that first year ended. In time, if both parties stay true to course, a comfortable, dependable kind of union will develop and endure. I no longer need to be told. I know.

Freedom is important in an enduring marriage. We have learned to give each other space to pursue our separate interests. After our son and daughter married and we became a couple again, we could also become individuals once more. My husband likes to treasure hunt in the woods around our house. I care not for treasure hunting but respect his hobby. Bill enjoys sports. I don't. I like poetry. He doesn't. Still, he occasionally listens patiently when I recite or read an especially beautiful turn of phrase in a poem. Marriage is a matter of give and take.

Some people love their pets, and their pets reciprocate. I know childless couples who have pets, and the pets become family members. For people who dislike animals, this may be hard to understand. Getting to know a pet and discovering that it has unique personality traits just like humans is part of what pet ownership is all about.

Then, there is the love of inanimate objects. I've never understood this kind of adoration. But the most dangerous kind of love is the obsessive love of money. A person can easily be transformed into a miser, a miserable person who lives for no reason other than to hoard more and more money.

Back to marital love and our forty-eighth wedding anniversary—my husband made reservations at Skeenie's hot-dog stand, where he promised me an unforgettable evening under the stars. Love is a many-splintered thing.

Joining the Old Boys' Club

A few years ago I was invited to join an organization that at one time had admitted only men. Talk about exclusive, it was exclusive with a capital E, and the members were proud of it. After all, belonging to an organization that picks and chooses is part of the fun of belonging. Since that exclusive attitude had been ruled unconstitutional, however, membership became non-exclusive; that is, it was opened to us women.

Excited about the invitation, I decided to join despite my having to fork out the considerable fees, payable every three months. I was sure that the weekly conversations at the round cloth-covered tables would be stimulating and more than worth the money. I would learn about stocks and bonds and about the secrets of success in the business world. In other words, I'd be networking with the best of the best, for I had heard that millionaires were plentiful in that group.

Looking sharp in my camel-colored suit, albeit minus a power tie, I attended my first meeting. I entered the large room where club members clustered in small groups around the room. Several of the men who saw me standing uncertainly by the door took great pains to greet and welcome me. Of course, I stood out in the crowd. They could tell right away that I was a member of a different kind, for I was the only woman among perhaps sixty men. I was looking forward to brilliant dialogue, remarks that would astound me with their depth. Most of all, though, I wanted to transform my business into a venture that would include corporate offices throughout the world. Belonging to the old boys' club would surely help to ensure that.

Why I remember the very noontime when a member with his expensive suit and red power tie smiled at me and said, "Dolly, I expect at each of our meetings there are at least thirty millionaires in this very room."

His remark triggered visions of seeing myself on my own yacht or in the south of France where maids catered to my every whim. Coming out of my reverie, I filled my plate from the buffet table and searched for a seat.

I soon settled in with about ten fellows seated at a table near the speaker's lectern. (That's how I got my cherished invitation. It came after I delivered a speech to the group a few weeks earlier.) As I picked at my food, I sharpened my listening skills and tuned in to the conversations. I didn't want to miss a golden word. Token or not, I became invisible at that table, though, for the discourse focused on football and hunting and golf and—all trivial matters when contrasted with the matter of becoming a millionaire. The next meeting and the third were the same. Shucks, I finally decided that I could stay at home and, for free, listen to our son talk about football and golf. He doesn't hunt, but I could live without talk of hunting.

Anyway, I've since discovered that old boys' clubs come in all shapes and sizes and, well, species, too. I know of several such cliques, and one consists of only two members whose names are Floppy Chenowith and Deacon Jones. Floppy, who doesn't even have to earn a living, lives high on the hog, as the saying goes. He eats scrambled eggs for breakfast and succulent roast beef for dinner. In nice weather when the sky is the color of bluebells on a sunny day, he lazes away his time lying in the yard or strolling along the skinny blacktop road that runs past his home. Deacon, who lives nearby with a minister and his wife, is Floppy's best friend, and these two dogs form their own old boys' club. They're not millionaires. They don't yearn for anything more than the necessities of life, but friendship is among those necessities. They're as wealthy as can be but don't have a penny to call their own. The next time I drive past the two old hounds, Floppy and Deacon, I'll smile and re-alize I made the right choice when I resigned from the first old boys' club. Two friends along a blacktop road have reminded me that I, too, am rich.

If the Shoe Flits

Walking from our living room to the kitchen, I was exhausted, and we have a small house. The journey felt like a two-mile hike up a steep mountain in three feet of snow. Here's why. My shoes kept flitting around be-neath my feet. I stepped out of one, then the other, backed up, slid my feet into each shoe again and again. By the time I reached the kitchen, I probably had walked two miles. Risa, my daughter, had advised me to "crunch" my toes. I did, but the crunching didn't help. Of course, the word "crunch" means to eat, and that's exactly what the toes must do. They must "bite" the insoles to keep the shoes on. In other words, I have to walk and think at the same time—not easy.

In the store, I looked at those shoes and had misgivings. They had no straps or leather around the back of the foot to hold them on. Still, almost all women seem to be wearing them these days. Even in restaurants, I see big naked toes and heels hanging out.

Back in the store, Risa said, "They're the latest thing, Mom, and they're so handy. You can just slide your foot in, and you're ready to go. That's why they're called slides."

I've since learned that they're also called mules, which has become a term for other things as well, but I'm discussing mules for the feet here. After Risa told me about toe-crunching, I decided to give the shoes a try.

I used to love shoe shopping, but entering a shoe department anymore is like entering a house of horrors or the shoe department of a Halloween costume store. There are shoes with big square heels and big square toes and thick soles. The heels alone are so heavy I can hardly lift the shoes. Most shoes are black and remind me of the hefty brogans men wear for hard outdoor labor. I wonder what the designers are trying to do to women. Before the clunky shoes came on the market, designers offered women shoes with pointed toes and spike heels. Now, the designers have gone to the other extreme. Today, we women can buy either brogans or slides. Where are the attractive, yet comfortable, shoes that are lightweight and will stay on the feet? Running shoes are lightweight, but the prices are as hefty as the heels on today's dress shoes. Besides, I'm not a runner.

Moving from toe to head, I was in a beauty shop one day, and a customer was talking about a friend, "Her hair looks like the hair-dos of the '50s. She needs to update."

I knew what updating meant. I see the "in" hairstyles worn by women television anchors. The hair looks as if it's been cut with a knife and fork. It must be stick straight and droopy. Droopy is the key word. No "big" hair or curly hair or wavy hair allowed. Occasionally, I see a woman clip all her long, straight hair to the back of the head with a large claw-like device, although she might also use a lace-covered elastic band. This procedure can be done in public and doesn't require a comb. It's fascinating to watch. In the meantime, sitting in the beauty shop (not to be confused with a pricey salon), I slumped lower in my chair because I was sure I had a '50s hairstyle.

I've thought a great deal about hairstyles and shoes lately and have decided, with respect to mules, if the shoe flits, bear it.

Just a Good Ole Girl

Because I'm qualified to run for an elective office, I think I will—in the next election. Here are my qualifications: I grew up poor on Brickyard Hill, which makes me just a good ole girl from a really humble background. My father's mother was a pillar in politics, hobnobbing with the powerful good ole boys. She was a vital part of the political machine if I ever saw one, all of which should count for something. What's more, my mother spoke the Appalachian dialect with pride and humor, a fact that further helps me to identify with my kind of people. Here's the clicker though: I'm an umpteenth-generation, genuine dyed-in-the-wool West Virginian, and, by golly, if that doesn't get it, I just don't know what will.

Here's my platform, which is as sturdy and steady as any platform I know. I promise not to begin a campaign letter with "Dear Senior Citizen." At the same time, I promise to take care of the old folks because I am old. I'll fight to get prescription drug costs canceled for everyone over sixty-five years old. This little ole country girl will go toe-to-toe with the big drug companies until they cry "uncle." I'm not sure whether I'll do my courageous fighting in Congress or in the Governor's office, but you can bet that whichever office I run for I'll fight, fight, fight.

As for education, I'll echo the cry that "no child will be left behind." To put this into practice, I'll make sure there are no lines of children on schoolyards or in school halls. Instead of standing in lines, students will always stand in circles. The desks in classrooms will also be placed in circles so that no child will be on the back row (that is, left behind) where his or her self-esteem might get crushed. You can see that I mean business.

As for the economy, I'll see to it that we pay good taxpayers' money to big companies that are on the brink of filing for bankruptcy. At no cost to the company that promises to enter our state for a short time, we'll do the remodeling, the infrastructure work, whatever these big companies need just so we can provide clerical, minimum-wage jobs for our good citizens in the beautiful state of West Virginia. To ensure our efforts for economic growth, we'll place even more "Certified Business Location" signs alongside our interstates.

To generate more money to expand a state government that already has moved into all buildings vacated by businesses that have moved to other states, we'll expand gambling. We'll have car races, horse races, dog races, even woolly worm races and every kind of gambling machine you can think of (oops, I mean gaming machines). Then, we'll set up a hot line to help those who become addicted to gaming. There is no end to the things that state government can do for its citizens when it generates enough money. Okay, there are some who say we're not generating money, that we're just taking from the poor and giving to the office holders for further dispensing. I'll debate that with my opponent.

Now to that all-important doctor shortage in our state. I have the solution, folks, and you're gonna love it. I'm going to place, free of charge, in every doctor's office one of those gaming machines in which gamers insert money and get nothing back. At the end of each month, the doctor can have all the money in his or her machine to pay the high cost of malpractice insurance.

Finally, I'll have an open-door policy and a phone system that's not automated so you don't have to press one, then two, and so on. Besides, I promise that you won't have to listen to music while you wait. May I count on your vote?

'Tis the Season

It's upon us, folks, whether or not we're ready, and we seldom are. We're in the midst of those hectic-filled days between Thanksgiving and Christmas when otherwise sane women become afflicted with a strange kind of madness. As a woman, I'm sorry to admit that men fare far better during this special season than we women. Men relax and watch football or play golf (weather permitting) or sit precariously atop trees in trendy tree seats as they watch for deer in the woods. Deer, by the way, are animals that know how to keep their feet on the ground unless, that is, they're leaping through the forest in an effort to escape being, uh, harvested.

Unlike men, most of us women have no idea how to relax. Here's a brief digression, an observation: I think women envy men's ability to be calm, carefree, serene. Conversely, I'll bet most men envy women's ability to rush around, find things, and get chores done. By first light, then, on Friday morning after Thanksgiving, we women have already worked ourselves into a virtual frenzy. It is precisely on the aforementioned Friday when the starting gates open, and if we're going to win the seasonal race, we must be out front.

By dawn on Friday, our eyes are little more than fiery BBs as we drive to the nearest shopping mall. There, greeted by countless other shoppers standing in long lines, we wait outside stores for doors to be unlocked. Of course, you won't find the Martha Stewart types elbowing their way around stores on the year's biggest shopping day. They have already hand-knitted, handcrafted, and home-baked every special gift on their list and long before Thanksgiving—a fact they like to share.

Gift buying or gift making is only the beginning. We must wrap those gifts in something, and not just any something will do. We agonize over whether to choose formal or country wraps. Should we use bags or boxes? Men who sometimes accompany us to stores remain forever relaxed, but they see us women as a collective, perpetual puzzle. Who cares, they wonder, about wrappings anyway. We women care, that's who. I don't know why. We just do. We're women.

My husband's idea of decorating is to toss one string of half burned-out lights over a bush and plug them in. He says it takes just ten minutes, and he's finished. No self-respecting woman would ever do that. We fret over every detail. Do our Christmas decorations match the living room décor? Is our theme consistent throughout the house? How about the outside lights? Are they consistent with the interior theme? And why did the husband string the lights along just one side of the bush? When the wife finds him to ask, he's napping. That's why he had to take a break. Naps are important to men. Are we envious? Yes, but we don't have time to think about it. Right now, you see, we're mad, mad, mad, for 'tis the season and we are, after all, women.

Holiday Greetings from the Withrows: A Spoof

Dear Friends,

It's time to catch you up to date on activities at our place during the past year, a year that has been kind to us, as you will soon learn. First, my husband was fleetingly tempted to leave his luxurious retirement when he received a call from a representative of the hundred billion-dollar corporation, Best Gidgets at Any Price. The caller asked my husband if he would be willing to serve as president. Unfortunately for the company, my spouse had to turn the offer down because, as he explained to the disappointed rep, he had already planned an African safari. After the safari, he will be designing his own beautiful air balloon. Once completed, the balloon will serve as his private mode of transportation as he floats around the earth. There have already been movie, television, and book offers, so it's going to be a really big event. Advertisers have promised to donate all profits to various charities of my husband's choice.

Our son is now CEO of two Fortune 500 companies because he can do twice the job in half the time at each corporate office. Speaking of offices, you should see his two office suites. One office has a wall that is a giant aquarium; the other corporate office boasts an eighteen-foot wall down which a gentle waterfall cascades. That's just the beginning, but I want to remain humble. There's nothing worse than a bragging generic letter, so I'll remain modest.

I cannot fail to tell you about our lovely daughter, though. She now owns international patents for her Creative Crafts, Inc. I tell you everything that girl touches turns to gold. In her spare time, she models her own designer dresses, and despite the seemingly untouchable prices, her clothes are always in demand by the rich and famous.

We have three handsome grandsons who also happen to be geniuses. As young as they are, they have already captured national attention because of their brilliance. They have even been offered full scholarships to Yale, Harvard, and Princeton, respectively. They continue to dazzle with talents to spare in music, art, biology, medicine, sports, English, foreign languages, and higher mathematics.

I would feel guilty if I were to omit mention of our dear pets. Our Australian cattle dog has learned how to understand several French words, after mastering English, and our French poodle is learning, of all things, Spanish. I tell you those animals never cease to amaze me.

Well, friends, it's beginning to look a lot like Christmas around our sixty-five-room mansion. Our halls are decked with live holly that Martha Stewart and I have nurtured throughout the year, and our home is just about ready for open house. The guest list includes family members and a thousand of our closest friends. And speaking of Martha Stewart, she and I have been working on a secret formula for mass-producing real snowflakes. Okay, so we've had the help of a few scientists, but Martha and I were the real brains behind the formula. Because of our combined efforts, I can assure everyone from coast to coast and from north to south that we can snow you in time for Christmas. So to one and all, from our house to yours, we wish you the happiest of holidays and a bright New Year filled with all good things.

Stealing the Show

No one can steal the show the way children can. One year, the children's Christmas musical was especially entertaining. People who don't attend children's church performances have no idea what they're missing.

The stage had been cleverly decorated with white helium-filled balloons, which emulated clouds. On the stage, a bleacher-like structure held four or five rows of little angels dressed in white robes. The smallest stood in the front row. A little girl, no more than three or four years old, began to get restless. Wearing a frilly dress with a gathered skirt, she twisted her upper body first to the right, then to the left. She pulled the skirt of her dress in the opposite direction with each twist, and with each twist, it went a little higher. She was having a grand time. Then, the little boy next to her became restless. He sat down with legs crossed and smiled at the audience. In the meantime, the tiny girl turned toward him, looked down, and gave him a wide grin. I was sure that I could see the flash bulb of an idea above her head. I did, for she then raised her skirt in front of her face and lowered it over his head. While this show was in progress, to the left, another small boy was preparing to dive headfirst off the stage, as if into a pool. I didn't know which show to watch. An amazing woman, the leader continued to smile and direct her choir of angels. Of course, it is those distractions that make Christmas programs memorable and hysterically entertaining.

Children not only grab the limelight on stage, but they also steal the show wherever they are. My grandson went to school and told his kindergarten teacher and the entire class that his family skinny-dipped together. No, no, they don't. Our daughter teaches a Sunday school class, and a four-year-old told her that his mother got a pistol out of her purse and shot their cat. Daughter Risa, after talking with the mother, discovered the family had neither a cat nor a pistol. When Risa asked her class where, according to the previous week's lesson, Jesus had been, one little boy said, "Jesus was at the zoo." Actually, Jesus had been in the synagogue, but *zoo* is easier to pronounce. The same three-year-old had told his parents that Risa was his "cutie-patootie."

A friend told me about a child's misinterpretation of the ending of a prayer. The child meant to say, "in the name of the Father, the Son, and the Holy Ghost." The child actually said, "in the name of the Father, the Son, and in the hole He goes."

Children in weddings are something else. One wedding I attended included a flower girl who had not wanted to wear the special dress purchased from afar. That was a bad omen. The little boy who would accompany her down the aisle was no more than a toddler. The girl's older sister was a maid of honor and stood by temporary, red-carpeted steps the girl was supposed to climb. She was then to walk toward the two matrons of honor, where she would stand during the ceremony. Instead of walking up the steps, she crawled, her ruffled panties aimed at the audience. She stood on the top step and jumped into the arms of her sister. That was so much fun. She did it three times. In the meantime, the toddler, who was supposed to stand with the best man and ushers, rushed to his mother, who was a matron of honor. She reached down, picked him up, and held him throughout the remainder of the service. Immediately after the last prayer, Risa, also a matron of honor, heard the mother say (with head still bowed), "Amen. He's wet his pants." But as Shakespeare knew, "All's well that ends well."

When All Else Fails

Every January, almost every American I know wants not only to be healthy but also to be fit. Little wonder. On Thanksgiving Day, we begin gorging ourselves and we don't stop until the New Year's party has ended. We awaken on New Year's Day and still must eat the requisite cabbage, black-eyed peas, and all the other foods (depending on location) that we believe will bring good health and prosperity throughout the coming year. Well, now, all this devouring of everything that hasn't moved gives us much the same shape as a party balloon blown to capacity with hot air. What to do? Why, we invest in fitness equipment; that's what we do. This means buying expensive items that must be (here it comes) assembled. That's an innocent-sounding word, but don't be fooled.

The only positive side of an assemblage get-together is the entertainment of bystanders who watch assemblers at work. Here's my story. Putting together a luxury treadmill, two assemblers began by opening the box. This in itself takes skill, strength and a large crow bar.

As soon as the box was opened and parts fell all over the floor like a spilled bag of cracked corn, Assembler One (called Will Knot Read, for I'm protecting the guilty here) said with a wrinkled brow and a lemon-like frown, "Some of the parts are missing."

Knowing Will, I'm aware that this is his first comment immediately after he opens a carton containing any product demanding hours of assemblage. Invariably, the product has hundreds of tiny packages each containing countless nuts, bolts, screws, wires, Parts A though Z, and countless big parts to be placed into countless little parts, none labeled with a letter. Letters of the alphabet are only on the direction sheet.

Assembler Two (a.k.a. Fred M. Patience) begins the assembly process. It isn't long until the inanimate objects, once resting quietly in a large dark carton, begin to take on human characteristics. Freddie says, "This treadmill is stupid, ridiculous. This is insane. We should return it and get our money back. That's what I'd do."

The treadmill doesn't answer, but it flaunts multicolored wires where wires should never be. They stick out the cracks and point straight at Freddie, who looks at steady-as-she-goes Will and says, "Why can't we just cut these wires off?"

"Well, go ahead," says Will, "but I doubt if it will run without those wires."

Impatient Freddie, by this time, has already left the wire problem and is trying to place a screw in a dark hole, but everything's upside down, so the screw keeps falling to the floor, all of which triggers another on-slaught of adjectives normally reserved for humans. This time the still-unassembled treadmill is stubborn, fool-ish, and ignorant. What's more, the usually steady Will is getting agitated and says, "Just do it anyway you want."

Rita N. Structions, an entertained onlooker, decides to help the workers. She says, "Freddie, you can't just look at the pictures. You have to look at the words, the words, Freddie. You have to read the instructions, too."

She proceeds to read instructions to the two assem-blers who continue to grumble. Here's my take on all this. Being healthy, being fit, having a fit, and being just one step ahead of a fit are all different. I hope in the coming year to be healthy, but I'll leave being fit to the world's great assemblers. Oh, be sure to look for yard sales, come spring. You're bound to find all sorts of fit-ness equipment for sale, and, hey, it will already have been assembled.

Three Stages of Love

When I was a young bride, I read something that shocked me and something I was too optimistic to be-lieve. I read that young love is one of passion, middle-aged love is one of habit, and old-aged love is one of dependence. Despite the dreary outlook of love's ever-changing nature, I've lived long enough now to know the truth in each of these three stages.

On Valentine's Day when I had been married six years, my husband (passionately in love of course) sent me a half-dozen red roses. Thrilled, I was sure that each of the following years I would receive an additional red rose symbolizing each additional year of our marriage. I just knew that on our twelfth Valentine's Day, I would have finally worked my way up to a whole dozen red roses. Those six, however, were the last flowers he ever sent. Had he persisted in buying an additional rose for each year of our wedded bliss, he would now have to hire an eighteen-wheeler to deliver my posies. The years passed, and we unwittingly moved into the next stage of love.

What with colic, diapers, and formulas, several Valentine's Days passed unnoticed by either of us. We were in the middle of our marriage and our habits included working from first light to last. When our son and daughter were in school and in a myriad of other activities, my husband and I didn't have time to give a thought to hearts and flowers. Our daily routines had by that time become habit, but it was a comfortable habit. When, on rare occasions, we were able to go out to eat, we felt easy enough with each other to dine without the need of constant chatter, the kind that young lovers must engage in to impress each other. We had already said it all and, by that time, could read each other's minds anyway. We were like coffee and cream, sun and summer. We just naturally went together, and we were in the second stage of easy-habit love.

The middle years of our marriage are gone, and with our son and daughter both married, my husband and I have once more become a couple. Before sweethearts' day this year, I looked in a card shop for an appropriate valentine but soon discovered that valentines today are aimed at nieces, nephews, siblings, parents, grandparents, teachers, and even trash collectors. How romantic can it be if all those folks need valentines from all of us folks? Also, flowers have lost their appeal.

My husband and I like sweets; we depend on them in the same way we depend on each other. Three weeks before Valentine's Day this year, I bought him a heart-shaped box of heart-shaped candy, mainly because I couldn't pass it up. We ate it the same day, each slipping pieces out of the box while the other was out of the room. By night, the entire box was empty, but we were full. The following week, my husband bought a box of Valentine's chocolates for me. Again, we secretly devoured each piece, and by the next day it, too, was gone. On February 12, I bought him more chocolates in a heart-shaped box, and we ate the last piece on February 14. Now, I've gained another five pounds along with lots of knowledge. Having experienced the three stages of love—passion, habit, and dependence—I've learned that each stage has its merits. Now, why didn't that maxim tell me that when I was a wide-eyed bride?

Building a Snowperson

It is safe to say that Indian summer has at last disappeared. Oops! I should have said that Native American summer has gone, leaving us with the pall of gray winter days except, of course, when the snow comes to cover the ground. Depending on your point of view, snow turns everything into a winter wonderland or wreaks havoc by creating slick roads. If the snow is wet enough, though, and we have the time, we can build a snowman. Oops! There I go again. Sorry, sorry, sorry. I mean we can build a snowwoman. No, that won't do either. Okay, so we can build a snowperson.

Talking and writing today have become increasingly difficult because the word wardens are out there listening and watching. Communicating was difficult before the word wardens (the WWs) came on the scene, but now trying to communicate with our fellow human beings is like trying to walk a tightrope without an umbrella.

It is best if we avoid using the word "man," especially if we're referring to both men and women. As a linguist, I understand that. I do. A mailman is now a mail carrier, and a stewardess is now a flight attendant. A fireman is a fire fighter, and a policeman is a police officer. I don't have a problem with that, but what do we call a manhole cover? Watch it now. And what about freshmen, those students in their first year of high school or college? Can we call them freshpersons? Does that change the meaning? I think so. Even the word *person* ends with—there it is again—*son*. It's always *person*, never *perdaughter*. The word *female* ends with—dare I say it?—*male*. *Mankind* has been rendered politically incorrect, so it's been replaced with *human kind*. Ah ha! Look at the last syllable of *human*. Yep, it ends with *man*. Even the word *woman* ends with *man*, and pluralize it, meaning lots of women, and the word ends with *men*. Why, shucks, there's just no way to rid the linguistic world of *man* or *men*.

Then there is another problem, which most of us are willing to accept because we want to be, um, sensitive. How do we deal with singular antecedents with pronouns that refer to them? Stay with me now, for I'm about to give an example that will make the preceding murky statement clear. Here it is: *Each reader brings his attitude to a piece of writing*. Notice how I used the word *his* when referring to *reader*. Since the reader might be male or female, I cannot do that anymore. I must use *his* or *her* as in the following sentence: *Each reader brings his or her attitude to a piece of writing*.

Several years ago, when sexist language was first discovered to be the bane of human kind, at least of womankind, one of my students, a male, wrote the following sentence: *I do not believe in premartial* [sic] *sex because he or she might get pregnut* [sic]. The entire essay was riddled with *he* or *she*, *him* or *her*, and *his* or *hers*. Well, now I began to wonder why that young man kept putting *he* in front of *she*. Was he a sexist? And he was trying so hard to be sensitive. Perhaps there's no way linguistically to appease everyone on the face of the earth, and when we try, we often muddle the message, rendering it indecipherable. I'm going to throw care to the winds, which are genderless, and venture out into the winter wonderland and build a snowperson.

The Shining Signing

It was what I called my Monica Lewinsky lipstick. After coating my lips with a small device that held bright red paint, I placed on my lips an overlay of gloss. The gloss was supposed to make my lips glisten and glimmer like tiny lights on bare-boned trees during the holidays. My shining lips, I reasoned, would help to lure potential buyers to my table at a book signing. The first challenge is to get people to see an author sitting behind his or her stacks of books. The second challenge is to get them to approach the table, however timid they may be.

Riding in the passenger seat toward a trendy bookstore where I was to sign books, I thought to look in the mirror to see if I needed more lip-gloss. Whoa! The lipstick had begun to crumble and cake, and part of the bright red had turned dark and was coating my front teeth. At first glance, my two front teeth appeared to be gone, blacked out. I worked on removing the lipstick from said teeth and once at the bookstore, I decided not to offer a wide smile. A tight little grin would have to suffice.

Once inside the store, I sat behind a card table that had been covered with a crimson cloth on which copies of *More than Penny Candy* were neatly displayed. I watched the parade of humanity pass by me. If they saw me, they pretended they didn't. I was contented for a few minutes because the store was a marvelous place for an author, for a reader. I was, after all, surrounded by the wonderful world of books. Also, I knew I was in the company of scholars, for they looked neither right nor left as they entered the store. Instead, they aimed straight for the trendy coffee shop. Once there, each ordered a favorite latte or cappuccino, sat at a table with a backdrop of funky art on the walls, and opened a book brought from home. These book gurus demonstrated no curiosity whatsoever in the treasures hidden between the covers of my *Penny Candy*. Shucks, I thought scholars were supposed to be curious about the world around them. It soon became apparent that my shining lips alone would not sell books. I would have to resort to another strategy. I began speaking to people, while offering my tight little smile and trying, at the same time, not to show my front teeth. My teeth have a way of displaying themselves when I talk, so my words had odd pronunciations, which, I think, finally stimulated the curiosity of the erudite. My mouth contortions, along with strange new words, drew people to my table at long last. That's when I forgot all about my teeth, my lips, my looks, and simply told true stories of how buyer after buyer of *Penny Candy* had returned to purchase as many as eight and nine additional copies for gifts. That's when I was able to tell my story of how one woman was going to put each of her eight copies into a basket with candy and a candy dish. She exclaimed, "My shopping will be finished and the recipients will love *Penny Candy*."

Once a small crowd had gathered around my little table, I told them other heart-warming experiences I've had with readers of my columns and of *Penny Candy*. The scholars sensed the truth and, at last, began buying copies. The trip to the bookstore for my very first signing of my third book was a shining success, all of which made me feel humble—very. I could have left the lip-gloss at home, for my readers—not the gloss—made the experience a shining signing.

PHOTO: CRAIG CUNNINGHAM

About the Author

Dolly Withrow is the author of three previous books: *"From the Grove to the Stars"* (the history of West Virginia State College), *"The Confident Writer"* (a grammar-based writing textbook for college students and writers in general), and *"More than Penny Candy"* (an essay collection). A columnist for *The Jackson Herald* and the *Charleston Daily Mail*, Dolly has won numerous writing awards, including a national award and the first-place award for her columns entered in the West Virginia Press Association's competition.

A retired English professor and grammarian, Dolly has taught for the University of Iowa's world-famous Summer Writing Festival. Since 1987, she has presented writing workshops for Fortune 500 companies, governments, and organizations. A popular public speaker, she spoke to the West Virginia Press Association members. As a result, she was invited to speak to the New York Press Association.

West Virginia Public Broadcasting airs her essays on its radio programs *"Inside Appalachia"* and *"Dateline: West Virginia."*